WITHDRAWN
The
Living
Together
Trap

The Living Together Trap

Everything Women and Men Should Know

Rosanne Rosen

New Horizon Press
Far Hills, New Jersey

Requests for permission should be addressed to:
New Horizon Press
P.O. Box 669
Far Hills, NJ 07931

Rosen, Rosanne.
  The Living Together Trap

ISBN: 0-88282-075-3
New Horizon Press

Manufactured in the U.S.A.

1997 1996 1995 1994 1993 / 5 4 3 2 1

to Sara Jane, Halley,
and Mark

Contents

Acknowledgments

The Living Together Trap reflects the joint effort of the hundreds of men and women who revealed their innermost joys, fears, heartaches, and disappointments to me and my sincere determination to present their stories in an honest and forthright manner. It is to these individuals that I owe my gratitude and want to say thank you. Without their time and willingness to share their lives so candidly with all of us, it would have been impossible to present this stark reality of live-in love.

I would also like to thank my publisher, Joan Dunphy of New Horizon Press, for her interest in this topic and Jeff Herman, my agent, whose continued efforts made this publication possible. My acknowledgments would be incomplete without thanking my husband, Mark, and my daughters, Sara Jane and Halley Rosen, for their support, which means so very much to me.

Discovering the Living Together Trap

A letter from a friend in her early thirties chronicled her two-year live-in relationship. The stationary did not need traces of her tears to convey the pain and anguish she was venting. Her descriptions of plotting uneventful jaunts past the local jewelry store to hint at the modest engagement ring she yearned for and her agonizing fear that she was quickly passing through her reproductive years unmarried powerfully tugged at my own heartstrings.

Not long after her letter arrived, I accompanied my husband on a business trip with a thirty-five-year-old male associate and his second young live-in partner. For several years I had witnessed the emotional public outbursts of his first and very recently deposed housemate, frustrated at their rocky relationship. When they split months before, I had a clear view of this man's heartbreak.

I became curious and couldn't help but wonder how many men and women were finding that live-in love did not proceed exactly as they imagined. I located candidates in their twenties, thirties, forties, and early fifties who were willing to divulge their most private feelings about their live-in relationships given the pledge of anonymity and confidentiality. Their motivations to meet me were varied. A young woman said at the end of our interview, "If I had a little sister, I would warn her about living together."

Speaking with me gave her the opportunity to do that for countless others. Men and women who had lived together and now appeared relatively comfortable in their married lives used the interviews to vent anger and frustration they still harbored for their spouses from their tumultuous live-in days. A twenty-seven-year-old man who was looking for answers to his current dilemma wanted the chance to verbalize his feelings in the presence of a good listener. And a few couples just enjoyed the chance to share the success of their live-in love relationship. Their stories were by far the minority of the tales I heard.

It quickly became apparent to me that the more prevalent patterns revealed unexpected perils and hazardous precedents that trap many men and women who opt to live together and sabotage their dreams of love or marriage. These insights are drawn from the meticulous examination of more than a hundred live-in relationships that primarily reflect the experiences of educated, middle-class Americans. For them more often than not, moving in posed a threat to their future happiness. *The Living Together Trap* reveals a realistic, in-depth look at live-in love that enables men and women to evaluate how cohabitation might affect their love relationship and how they can avoid the trap that potentially awaits them moving in. Using this information wisely should enable them to gain greater fulfillment over the course of their relationship.

The first six chapters clearly expose the men and women who are at greatest risk in live-in relationships and illuminate the situations that entrap them. Chapter 7, "The Best of Live-In Love," uncovers the optimal conditions for successful and fulfilling cohabitation and takes a look at several couples who found living together to be positive and beneficial for their relationship. Chapter 8, "Programming for Success," offers twenty important questions to ask oneself before moving in and the do's and don'ts of cohabiting. Since marriage is on the minds of the majority of individuals who live together, Chapters 10 and 11 reveal who is most likely to get to the altar and the steps they take to maximize the potential for marital success. Because the outlook for long-lasting happiness living together can be questionable, it is only fitting that the last two

chapters outline the necessity for protecting one's rights and interests not covered by law and provide a five-point plan for moving
out and moving on.

It is my sincere hope that *The Living Together Trap* will benefit
those individuals whom I had the pleasure of meeting and interview-
ing while researching this book, those who were looking for answers, and all of the other men and women who seek lasting
happiness but are caught in the trap of live-in love.

CHAPTER 1

A Seductive Bill of Goods

The myth of live-in love that eager buyers often impulsively purchase reads like a romance novel, sugar-coated with fairy tales. The fervor of passion and the promise of happy endings are deliciously appealing. Few signs of the troublesome reality are visible before the neatly packaged popular fantasy is unwrapped and couples find themselves on an emotional roller-coaster ride.

To reduce this risk requires a candid look at the reasons men and women opt for live-in relationships and how their expectations stack up against what they get. This exploration reveals many discrepancies that often engender hazardous precedents, a perpetual state of limbo, and the loss of power and self-esteem—particularly among women. Only after the perils of live-in love are fully shown will it be possible for men and women to assess the romanticized expectations, the hidden agendas, and true realities of the love or marriage relation they seek.

WHO ARE THE EAGER BUYERS?

Over the last ten years, the number of unmarried heterosexual couples who live together has jumped 80 percent in the United States. Today that represents more than three million American couples. The largest proportion of them, 56 percent, have never been married, and approximately one-third of all live-ins have been divorced. Forty-five percent of all women in the United States between the ages of twenty-five and thirty-four have at one time been live-in partners. The figures for men are comparable.

The trend toward cohabitation is taking hold in European countries as well. The number of British women between the ages of eighteen and forty-nine who have had live-in relationships doubled from 1979 to 1987, and 11 percent of the women between eighteen and twenty-four have opted to try moving in. These statistics are consistent with surveys of French women but lower than those in Finland, Norway, and Sweden.

WHAT IS ON THE SHOPPING LIST?

For many of these eager buyers, moving in occurs as spontaneously as the lovemaking that sparks the idea of living together—and is just as irresistible. "I'm not sure how it happened; it kind of evolved" is a common refrain of live-in lovers.

Despite the lack of purposeful analysis before moving in, most buyers anticipate purchasing:

- a satisfying and secure relationship
- a committed monogamous partner
- financial and sexual perks
- a ticket to matrimony
- a replica of a marriage relationship
- a clean, carefree split from their partner in the event that they do no get the goods they are after.

LIVE-IN LOVERS

This sounds easy enough, but a more in-depth look at four major groups of live-in lovers, their basic agenda, and their purchases begins to expose the trap that has caught a large number of men and women.

Marriage Seekers

In a 1989 study 70 percent of the women surveyed who moved

in with a man had marriage on their minds. They either saw living together as the means by which to entrap a hesitant lover into becoming a marriage partner, a way to prove their compatibility, or a step in the natural progression toward the altar.

Pricilla does not deny it. "Marriage was my goal. Mark had just gotten a divorce. I thought it was good strategy to move out of town and away from his ex. I followed him to Boston and moved in. If I didn't, I was afraid I would lose him and that we wouldn't get married. If I went with him, I felt I could convince him that I was the right woman for him."

Elizabeth used the promise of living together as the leverage she needed to get engaged. "Clark asked me to move in. I refused. I told him once we were engaged I would. I thought that would push him into marrying me sooner. We lived together for six months before we got married."

The marriage theme even resonates among the live-in buyers who comprise the remaining categories. These men and women may not be as blatant or calculating in their attempt to move on to matrimony, but the notion invariably lurks in their minds.

Mutual Users

Mutual users usually move in together after knowing one another only a short period of time and before a significant emotional attachment or love relationship develops. The possible benefits garnered from living together are readily apparent. Many users are motivated by one or more of the following gains.

Convenient and Plentiful Sex

"We were spending every night together. Pretty soon I had more of my clothes at her house than at my own. It was just easier to move in," admits Sam and a multitude of other men and women without future plans for their relationships.

"It was a fling with Ted," says Ellen. "Living together was just so we could enjoy each other. I was extremely physically attracted to him."

Some psychologists and therapists believe that all live-in

relationships are based solely upon a sexual relationship. While the sexual component is undoubtedly a major part of the package, the individuals I spoke with had a whole list of other benefits on their mind.

A Dollar Bonus

"It probably started out as a sexual relationship," admits twenty-seven-year-old Richard, who has lived with twenty-six-year-old Patsy for four years. "But the whole thing was mutually beneficial in an economic sense. Patsy wanted to move to Chicago but could not afford to on her own. Moving in with me made it possible for her to leave her parents' home. We split everything fifty-fifty, and within a year we moved into a larger and much nicer apartment."

"I suppose part of it was economics," Dominick, a man of forty, reveals hesitantly, describing the conditions that prompted him to share an apartment with Mary after knowing her for only two months. "I was going through a divorce. I had to move into my own place and money was tight. Mary was paying a lot for a one-bedroom apartment. Together we had enough furniture to fill up a bigger apartment and more comfortably afford the rent."

Regardless of age, economic enticements play a prominent role when mutual users decide to move in. Here romance easily gets confused with being able to afford a larger apartment, eating out, and VCRs.

The Companionship Factor

"I didn't know too many people in Cleveland. I was twenty-three and I had just moved there," explains Ken. "I met Polly, who was a few years older than me, and we started to date. Living together just seemed like the natural thing to do at the time. I never liked coming home to an empty house, and with Polly there I had a companion. With everyone so mobile today, I think loneliness plays a big part in deciding to live with someone. Marriage was not on my mind."

Caretakers and Nurturers

The young men to whom I talked and who admitted to this one are straightforward and honest: "My buddies and I are looking for mothers, women who take care of us," they say.

That sounds a lot like what Ken wanted when he said, "Meals are the worst. I hate to cook." Polly got that job.

And what about Richard, who foots most of the bills? "What do I like best about Patsy? She is very caring, very nurturing, and a great cook. Yea, she makes me feel cared for."

Romantic Roomies

Romantic images, a greater degree of emotional involvement, and many of the same benefits sought by other categories of mutual users entice couples to become romantic roomies.

"We did play house for a while. It was fun, and I liked it for about a year," recalls Val, twenty-six at the time of this live-in episode. "He kind of charmed his way into my house. He wanted to live with me to prove he could be a good mate, but it turned out he was more emotionally invested in the relationship than I was. He wanted to get married. I didn't. I was really enjoying the relationship and buying time. I knew he was a great housekeeper, but I knew things wouldn't work forever."

Alexis, age twenty-six, explains her year-and-a-half live-in relationship a little differently. "I wasn't sure if I was in love with Bill even though he was in love with me. I did like the intimacy of our relationship and the commitment we made to spend time together. I enjoyed living with him. I have roomed with different women and found this much more satisfying. We bought things together, decorated the apartment, and entertained like we were married. Living together was fine. I'm not sure, however, if the relationship was," she concludes.

Garth, who is forty-eight, says, "After my divorce I wanted a woman whose eyes got real big when she saw me." That was what he found several years ago in Sybil, fifteen years his junior, who fell madly in love with him and wanted to get married. "I tried to explain to her that this was a temporary relationship even though we had tremendous passion for each other and had fun living together. She fit into my life neatly."

True Believers

True believers are those men and women who:

- want a serious love relationship
- prefer living together to tying the knot
- do not see any difference in the quality of the two relationships
- have absolutely no interest in marriage
- voice concrete reasons why marriage is taboo to them.

The problem is that it is very difficult to find a *true* true believer.

Just when you think you have identified a true believer, he or she turns around and gets married. Celebrities regularly make the tabloids with this sort of news. Christopher Reeves supposedly never married the mother of his two older children because of scars from his parents' divorce. What happened to those same scars when he married the mother-to-be of his third child? You don't have to be in the public eye to have a change of heart.

Only a very small percentage of the men and women with whom I talked oppose marriage as a matter of principle. It quickly became apparent from my interviews that true believers of varying degrees were more likely to be motivated by individual needs and past experience than by philosophical purity.

A Believer of the First Degree

First-degree true believers put the thought of marriage out of their minds. They are completely satisfied within the framework of live-in love. The idea of marriage as the "tie that binds" runs counter to the core of their personality.

An example of one such relationship was Charles and Roberta. Charles was Roberta's first live-in lover.

"He was extremely intelligent and a tremendous companion," explains Roberta, a very attractive and intensely independent middle-aged woman. They parted as friends after five years when Roberta found Alan, who she felt was the love of her life.

"I never was nor am I now looking to get married," Roberta asserts. "There is nothing that marriage could do to make what Alan and I have any better a relationship. Alan and I *choose* to be together every day. I want us to be together but I also want to be free and unencumbered. It is my basic personality. I am a gypsy. For four years I lived in a hotel with all of my belongings under the bed. Security is not something I am looking for."

Alan, equally attractive and intelligent, concurs that his love for Roberta will last a lifetime . . . with or without marriage.

"She is one-hundred-percent self-sufficient. She knows exactly what direction she is going in. For her that is security. To try and penetrate that would be to take away her security."

True Believers of a Lesser Degree

Bob is representative of a contingent of youthful true believers who have become disillusioned with the institution of marriage. Reacting to the high divorce rate, the dissatisfaction with matrimony expressed by friends and family members, and his own marital failure, Bob doubted that matrimony still represented a permanent, fulfilling lifestyle.

Nonetheless, when his live-in lover became pregnant, he decided to marry. Children seem to be the turning point at which these lesser true believers surrender their beliefs. There was practically a consensus by this group that if and when they had children, they would marry.

Temporary True Believers

How can you be a true believer on a temporary basis? Ask Flo, a fifty-three-year-old woman married for twenty-six years and divorced for five before she and Adam moved in together almost three years ago. She won't hesitate to tell you that nothing is missing in her love relationship with Adam that a piece of paper would change.

"I don't feel any different living together than I did married. We think of ourselves as married. I am secure because he loves me."

But if she had her druthers, she says, "We would like to be married. I believe that two people who live together should be married. I'd like to celebrate the fact that we love each other."

So what's in the way? A very substantial monthly alimony check that would not be forthcoming if she married. "As I see it, this money is my pension. I earned it over twenty-six years. If and when my ex retires or dies, Adam and I will get married. A lot of people in our age bracket live together because of these types of financial complications."

There is a sizable portion of the senior and pre-senior population who live together instead of marrying to avoid loss of Social Security payments and other income derived from widowhood. A 1983 study showed that approximately one-fourth of the men and one-fifth of the women over sixty-five have lived with a partner outside of marriage.

EXPLODING THE MYTHS, OPENING THE BAG

After the bag of live-in love is open, the once-eager buyers are not always pleased with what they find inside. Women express the greatest dissatisfaction. Seventy-one percent of the women interviewed stated that after testing the waters once or twice, *they would not live-in again.* Of the women who conceded they might be tempted, the majority qualified their responses: They would move in only if the relationship was extremely serious and the prospect of marriage nearly certain.

Discovering the discrepancies between the imagined and the real state of live-in love sheds a new light on the fairytale myths that influenced significant numbers of both men and women to take the step to move in.

Pros and Cons at a Glance

Live-in lovers who got what was on their shopping list with relatively little anguish or conflict frequently acclaim the pros of living together. They enjoyed companionship, sex, and romance. More often than not they raised their standard of living. If they were unusually perceptive or cunning, they learned a great deal about their partner and either found true love or split without legal or emotional hassles.

Unfortunately, a significant number of couples got more than they bargained for. For starters, they complained about having to give up space, privacy, and control over their lives, possessions, and incomes. *Women in particular noted that they suffered a loss of self-esteem and became confused in the face of unsuccessful live-in relationships.*

While on an airline flight, I approached Tess, a pretty, young stewardess who I was told was having a live-in relationship. I asked if we could set up a time to talk, and she immediately responded with a question: "Are most of the people you talk to unhappy?" I had to admit that I had conducted a large number of interviews with teary-eyed women.

Taking Your Chances

It would have been telling only half the truth if I did not explain that while the majority of people I met gave living together the thumbs-down after trying it, there was a group for whom living together had served the intended purpose. Those who represent the best of live-in love will be introduced later as helpful guides to springing the trap.

The difference, it seems, between them and the stewardess was a matter of luck, know-how, experience, focus, and vision grounded in reality.

What are the chances of succeeding in live-in love on a permanent basis or moving on to a lasting marriage? According to a 1988 survey by the National Center for Health, no better than fifty-fifty. Even those statistics may be too optimistic. What they don't reflect are the tribulations and rocky marriages that often follow in the wake of living together.

◆   ◆   ◆

Who Said What about Sex, Monogamy, and Commitment?

Sex

In my interviews I found it not unusual to hear complaints about the sex life one envisioned versus the one that actually materialized. There are plenty of guys who agree with Ralph's assessment of the situation: "You move in to make sex more convenient and think your sex life will be great. Mine got worse."

"If it weren't for the threat of AIDS, I think sex would be better if I were just dating around," claims forty-year-old Randy, divorced and living with a woman for a year and a half. "Sex at home isn't all that good."

Kevin, age twenty-seven, admits, "What attracted me to her in the beginning was sex. There was a willingness to do whatever I asked. That has changed over a period of time. Sex is humdrum or nothing at all."

Monogamy

Many of the men I surveyed who are in a live-in relationship are not monogamous. Women too have extra-live-in affairs.

"There. I am not proud of it, but there were two or three times I slept with someone while Polly was away," recalls Ken. "I had guilt feelings, but I remember saying to myself, 'I'm not married. I can do this.' Now that I am married (to someone else), I have a totally different attitude."

"Bill was wonderful," begins Esther. "He put me on a pedestal, but it was suffocating. When we first moved in, I thought he was a great guy and that I loved him on some level. But I became attracted to someone else at work after six months. That is what really caused our breakup. I knew it was stupid and mean after a while. Finally I just told him I couldn't live with him anymore. I never told him about the affair."

Commitment

Very few of the men and women I surveyed gave commitment

as a reason for moving in. Without a significant commitment, men or women can't be certain who will lower the boom on their live-in relationship . . . or when, why, or where.

For instance, Daniel makes no pretense of where his relationship with Sara stands. "I just take everything one day at a time. As we go along, if she found someone else or I didn't like the arrangement, then I would understand and accept it. I hope she would do the same. If I met a woman and we had a great attraction to each other, I would pursue her."

The Significant Other: How Significant?

For some the title *significant other* expresses too little. Here's a pair to whom it expresses too much. This is not a unique story. It shines light on a common problem:

Leslie describes her relationship with Max, a number of years her senior, divorced, and a part-time custodian of his teenage daughter: "I dated Max two full years before I moved into his home. I was divorced and in my early thirties at the time. I had lived with him less than a year when his cousin's wedding became a major issue. The parents of the bride had visited us several months earlier. I welcomed them in Max's home and helped wine and dine them. I could hardly believe it when they invited Max and his daughter but not me to the wedding.

"Max's attitude was, 'What do you want me to do? It's not my affair.' Well I guess I wanted him to pick up the goddamned telephone and say, 'Why didn't you invite Leslie? I'm not coming unless she does.' I saw us as a couple. Evidently he and his family didn't. That weekend I stayed home and took care of his house and his dog.

"I thought the next weekend he would take me away *alone* to make up. But instead he gave in to his daughter's demands that he chaperone her and her friends on a weekend trip. He invited me, but I declined. I moved out shortly after that."

The Question of Marriage

It *can* be done. You *can* get your bride or groom—even though fewer than one out of every two couples pair off successfully in an enduring marital relationship after living together. The reality that the remainder of the participants discover is a difference in timetables, mistaken intentions, and inaccurate readings of compatibility tests.

Different Timetables

It is not uncommon for women, and especially men, to use living together as a tactic to delay marriage. For instance, one woman to whom I spoke, Elizabeth, may have gotten her man eventually, but here is what her husband had to say: "I didn't want to give up all my freedom yet, even the freedom to be with other women. I knew that I loved Elizabeth and wanted to marry her, but I also wanted to buy some time. I got engaged so that she would live with me and I wouldn't have to get married right away."

Samantha was not as lucky as Elizabeth. Two weeks before Christmas I was at a wedding where Samantha and her live-in beau, both in their mid-twenties, caught the bridal bouquet and the garter. With flowers in hand she said to me, "I hope this is an omen. Maybe Randy will surprise me for Christmas and get engaged."

There were no surprises for Samantha, at Christmas or at any other time. Randy had no intention of marrying her.

Mistaken Intentions

Absolutely nothing should be taken for granted in live-in love. Margie will attest to that. She had every reason to believe that she and Fred would marry. They had talked about it as high-school sweethearts. She had few reservations when he moved in to share her New York apartment during their college days. However, after several years of in-house duty, college diplomas on the wall, and an abortion, Margie became extremely concerned over when the ring was coming. She broached the subject, thought he needed time to get used to the idea, and waited.

Fred had other intentions. "I'm not getting married," he said rather easily. However, he wasn't at all opposed to continuing their relationship the way it was. His response so astounded Margie that it took a while for the truth to sink in and for her to move out.

Ten years have past, and Margie is finally getting married—but not to Fred. He is still single, although two more live-in lovers have passed through his portal.

Poor Compatibility Testers

If the object for many couples is to take a trial run before marriage, they are surprisingly poor testers. *Couples who live together before marriage divorce at a higher rate than those who did not, according to several studies.* The likelihood of divorce during the first two years of marriage is three times greater for those who do cohabit. After ten years of marriage, 38 percent of the couples who cohabited divorce, compared to 27 percent who lived together only after marriage.

Some social scientists believe that the statistics reflect the less traditional, less conforming attitudes of those individuals who opt for live-in relationships and who, therefore, are less troubled by the idea of divorce. However, the vast majority of women and men I spoke to would not be classified as nonconformists or individuals less likely to be affected by social mores. They were on the whole educated men and women with middle- to upper-middle-class incomes and traditional lifestyles and values. In a large number of cases, the reason marriages turned sour had more to do with not knowing how to take the compatibility test or how to set proper precedents for their partnership.

Marriage in a Class of Its Own

"Living together is just like being married." Everyone has heard that statement authoritatively uttered by men and women, far too many of whom have no experience with married life. The only fair way to evaluate this popular myth is to see what men and women who have been happily married and who have experienced live-in relationships have to say.

The Man's Point of View

Tom ought to be an expert. He lived with Ann and then Susan

and then Betty. He married Betty and is living happily ever after. "It's the old story—that commitment makes a world of difference," he explains. "If you are truly honest with yourself and committed to a marriage, you aren't hiding anything in the back of your mind. When you live with someone it is easy to think, 'If this doesn't work, I'm out of here.' My commitment to marriage is different than that."

Spoken like the true lawyer that he is with multiple experiences, Mike says, "I think there is a big difference between living together and being married. Living together is inherently unstable. Either it has to progress to a marriage relationship or it is going to fall apart and be unsuccessful. I don't think it is realistic to expect a live-in relationship to persist indefinitely. It is missing a formal commitment, a contract, and an unequivocal understanding by both partners that they are committed to each other."

Gregory was married for twenty years before his wife declared she was no longer in love and asked for a divorce. Involved in an on-going live-in relationship for a year and a half now, Gregory says that both living arrangements offer him the structure his life needs. He likes having an available partner and a predictable, orderly lifestyle. But there are limits to his live-in's authority that did not apply to his former wife.

"Living together is like being married on a day-to-day basis but implies more freedom and a different relationship than marriage," Gregory suggests. "I do not view Roz as part of my family as I did my wife. Consequently, I don't feel it is appropriate to consult her in my long-range plans. Actually, I get annoyed when she calls the office and asks me when I'll be home. I don't think I should have to account for my whereabouts or spend all of my leisure time with her. On the other hand, I don't expect her to do the things that my wife did for me. I do my own laundry and run my own errands. Naturally we each take care of our own finances."

Alan, married and divorced, lives with Roberta. Remember, she is the truest true believer I ran across. But even Alan with his sense of humor has something to say in favor of marriage and has fun telling his associates at work the truth about his relationship: "I have worn out my knees asking Roberta to marry me."

What does Alan want that he doesn't already have? He is practical in noting their inability to share each other's professional benefits and job perks that would be available if they were married. Besides, he says, "Not being the traditional couple presents a few minor irritations. No matter what the ties are between us, in the office they still consider me single. There is a perceived difference between me and the married guys. Roberta and I call each other partners, but it is a little awkward to express that on name tags at company functions. People would be a lot more comfortable if we were married."

The Woman's Point of View

Even though a true believer, Roberta concedes, "By the time I am seventy-five, I may be tired of referring to Alan as my boyfriend."

Women, like men, acknowledge the difference between live-in relationships and marriage. They find the latter more satisfying and secure. For example, Libby says, "Living together was like dating and going to bed with Frank. It was not like our marriage. We are responsible for each other now and share the same commitment to make our marriage work. I think it is easier to plan future goals. When you live together you don't really have a common ground to work toward."

Karen, a self-confident educator, remarks, "I feel safer being married." Part of her previous insecurity resulted from the perception Martin's professional associates had of the status of wives versus live-in partners. "When Martin and I would attend a legal meeting, the women lawyers and wives looked at me as a more or less temporary entity. Now that we are married, I sense a difference in their attitude toward me. They know I'll be around."

Flo, the fifty-three-year-old temporary true believer, encountered the same prejudice. But the perpetrator was the law. "Legally I am a nobody," she admits. "This is one of the disadvantages of not being married, and it bothers me. Adam was taken to the hospital and was in intensive care. I couldn't sign any of his papers. I couldn't even get in to see him without lying and stating that I was his wife. In our minds we couldn't be closer, but in the legal sense I am not his immediate family."

Hank is not a member of Linda's family either and poses a problem when it comes to her two sons, ages fifteen and eighteen. "If we were married," says Linda, "I would expect Hank to take a more cooperative and participatory role with my sons. My boys see him as my boyfriend, not a step-father. There is a big difference to my sons, and they let him know that."

Janice, a mature and bright woman in her mid-forties with an eleven-year marriage behind her and a current live-in lover, still prefers a marital relationship. "Even though I didn't have a good relationship in my first marriage, I thoroughly enjoyed the state of matrimony. I liked feeling secure and presenting ourselves as a couple to the world."

Why hasn't Janice exchanged her present status for matrimony? That is a subject for Chapter 4, "The Stalemate of Live-In Love."

Calling It Quits: A Tough Assignment

Moving out is one of the hardest things to do, state live-in lovers. Neither men nor women escape the pain, conflict, or guilt.

"Trying to break off my live-in relationship is harder than getting my divorce," declares Brent.

Tara doesn't know about divorce, but she sure knows about splitting up with her live-in when she was twenty-four. "It would have been a more lighthearted relationship if we hadn't lived together. I know that the majority of the relationship was about sex and having fun, but still I thought we would get married. When I moved out after two years, I flipped out. I had a nervous breakdown. I went into a depression. I couldn't sleep or eat. I called my father every hour, crying."

Ending a live-in relationship for Lee, a sensitive young man, posed a significant problem. "There is no question about it: It is more difficult to break up if you are living together than dating. You put yourself in a bad position. If you are the kind of guy who says, 'Get the hell out of here!' it's probably easy. But if you are trying not to rock the boat, it's hard. I felt I would have been the bad guy to go out and find another place. I kept saying to myself that maybe it would work out. I give Sue most of the credit for resolving my problem. She took the bull by the horns when she too realized we should separate. It would have taken me much longer to break up. Although it was mutual, it was painful to split. At times I felt rejected and thought I should try to get back together."

The moral of all these tales is: Don't expect to pack your bags and wave a friendly, nonchalant good-bye.

FACING THE POTENTIAL TRAP
OF LIVE-IN LOVE

Not everyone falls into the trap, but no one escapes the potential for danger. To see if you are becoming dangerously close, take the following test:

	Yes	No
Has living together fulfilled your initial object?		
Are you happier now than you were living alone?		
Do you feel more and more secure about your relationship?		
Are you better off financially than you were on your own?		
Is your sex life more than satisfactory with your live-in partner?		
Do you think you have a loyal, committed partner?		
Are *you* a loyal, committed partner?		
Do you share your partner's views on live-in love and marriage?		
Are you and your partner aiming the relationship in the same direction?		
Do you have complete trust in your partner?		
Are you satisfied being in a monogamous relationship?		
Would you move in with the same partner again?		

Add up all the yeas and nays. Any checkmark in the "No" column is cause for concern that you may be dangerously close to falling into the trap.

Fine-Tuning a Clear Picture

Though the dangers of live-in love should be well within view, the picture is not nearly complete or clear enough yet. The next five chapters will elaborate on those who face the greatest risk, how they become entrapped, why they were unable to disengage themselves from painful relationships, and how live-in love adversely affects the odds for a satisfying marriage partnership.

CHAPTER 2

Risky Business for Women

There are no guarantees when it comes to matters of the heart. However, among the women interviewed, there is a group who seem to have a propensity for heartache and are at greatest risk when moving in. They dramatically increase the chances for unrequited love and misery by ignoring brilliant red warning signs that suggest they are headed for trouble.

WHO ARE THE WOMEN AT RISK?

Women at greatest risk when moving in make costly trades and put themselves at a distinct disadvantage in a relationship. They trust their lover too much and aren't nearly skeptical enough. The woman at risk usually exhibits one or more of these common symptoms:

- lack of sufficient experience in love relationships
- fledgling understanding of how a healthy couple interacts
- questionable motive for moving in
- significant, disruptive change in her personal life
- fear of not finding love
- rose-colored outlook
- giving and nurturing personality
- floundering sense of self-worth.

Consequently, all too often these women find themselves caught in a relationship that:

- diminishes their fragile self-esteem
- clouds their good judgment
- causes them to temporarily lose control over their own destiny
- encourages them to hand over financial resources
- makes them put their needs second to those of their lover's
- creates an unhealthy dependency
- prompts them to give much more than they receive
- precludes easy exit
- comes with regrets.

And when the relationship is all over, these are the women who ask themselves, *"How could this have happened to me?"*

THE WORST SCENARIOS FOR WOMEN

Looking *in* as an objective observer rather than *out* as an active participant offers an unobstructed view into the deepest, darkest crevices of risky situations. Heed the warnings of the women who have experienced these tales of woe. They will undoubtedly help others to escape their jeopardy.

Don't Look for Love on the Rebound

Few men or women are strong enough to successfully handle love on the rebound. April is no exception.

Lonely and Suffering

April's story began twelve years ago, when her marriage of eleven years ended. She was devastated and lonely with two children in a new, large suburban home. "No one knows how badly I really suffered," she says. "I knew my husband was having an affair. I kept asking myself if it was my fault and what I had done wrong.

"Six months after we separated, I went home to visit my family in Cleveland and met Trent. It wasn't hard to fall for him. I had been so neglected sexually and emotionally. He paid a lot of attention to me and made me feel good. Two days after I went back to Detroit, Trent flew in and took me to lunch and asked me to go away with him. I said okay if I could take the children. No problem. He loved my boys from the beginning. We ended up taking a cruise on his fifty-two-foot yacht and dating exclusively.

"Several months later, when my divorce was final and I got a ton of money from my settlement and the sale of my house, Trent must have been able to smell it. His financial situation had plunged suddenly. He was always working on a deal, but nothing ever panned out. He was a deal maker who liked to live first class," describes April, trying to be flip at the same time she is chain smoking and laughing nervously.

"I moved back to Cleveland. I wasn't thinking clearly. I bought a duplex. He moved into one side rent-free, and I moved into the other. After a year and a half I thought he should move in with me so that I could rent out the other half. It made more sense. It cured my loneliness and gave me a new sense of security. I provided Trent with a lot and created a nice home atmosphere for him," she admits, embarrassed.

"I trusted Trent completely. Looking back, it seems ridiculous. I wanted to marry him but never said anything about it. I guess I was afraid he might leave me, and I wasn't ready for that. Now I see I had him move in to get over my husband. It was paramount in my mind to prove that I could make it work because I had failed at my marriage. I waited on him hand and foot. It was like there isn't anything I can't handle. Just give me a couple hours' notice and I can have dinner for one hundred.

"We lived together for about two years and traveled a lot. We went through all of my settlement, hundreds of thousands of dollars. I feel like I bought him off. I take the blame for squandering the money, but he surely set me up for it. He still owes me $30,000," acknowledges April.

Why did April spend so much money on Trent? "I was alone. I had these little kids, actually two babies. I was broken up. I thought my divorce was going to kill me. My husband never had time for me. With Trent, I had the money and he had the time."

In the end, Trent betrayed her. "I found out he had called up a friend of mine and asked her for a date," April explains. "I packed up and moved to South Carolina and had an affair with his best friend to get back at him. It was my tough luck I ran into him. That is all I can say. I should have taken time to think! My mind wasn't straight at the time. Isn't it remarkable that I can now laugh at all of this?"

Don't Be Lured by Baubles and Bangles

The older man and the promise of riches is an old recording that keeps getting rewound.

Too Much for a Small-Town Girl

Glenda, mature beyond her twenty-seven years, has a striking and imposing presence. It may have been what attracted Seth, a wealthy businessman more than twenty years her senior. For several months, Glenda refused to accept a date with him. She intuitively knew he was going to be hard to handle for a small-town girl. But after seven months she could not resist his elaborate offers and agreed to make their first date a whirlwind vacation that lasted two weeks.

"When I said I have to get back to my job," she reveals, "he wrote me a check for $2,000." What started out as an obvious sexual exchange ended up as a total change in lifestyle for Glenda. At the end of three months she sold her boutique, got engaged, and moved in with Seth. During their four-year engagement, as the wedding dress hung in the closet, they ended up canceling the ceremony several times over trivial arguments.

Looking back, Glenda justifies her decision to follow Seth to Texas and recounts the peril that followed. "We lived in separate states, and I knew that I couldn't afford to be where he wasn't if I wanted to succeed in wrapping him round my finger. I should have moved to Dallas but not into his home. I gave up my entire life. I severed my past. I can't really describe the loneliness I felt and how I put up with him for four years. I was consumed by him. You see, I came from a very poor background. I was tired of being in a small town, and this was a way out for me.

"I thought he was crazy about me. His entire intention was to overwhelm me. He was a controlling, manipulating, and domineering man, but I was too enthralled by what he offered me to see that. I even accepted his sexual peculiarities, and now I realize that once he found a woman who was willing to go through such elaborate schemes to satisfy him he was reluctant to let her go. On weekends I was to be available for lengthy sexual sessions. It could take a whole weekend to make him come. It was grueling work. I was his maid and prostitute. I was to have his meals on the table, and I wasn't allowed to go out when he was at home.

"Just the same, I felt so devoted to him because he gave me a certain security I have never known. I really enjoyed being with him in many ways, and I trusted him. He was generous as far as the holidays went, buying me jewelry and rings. However, he would give me only enough to run the house—not a cent more. He would keep telling me, 'You can't make it on your own.' He wanted me to be dependent on him and wouldn't let me work. I was a girl who had worked twelve hours a day before. I had no sense of who I was anymore. He tried to make me believe that I had total control over him and that I should enjoy that power.

"I tried to break it off three times. The first time, he booted me out of the house. I went home to my mother without any money. She couldn't help me. I went back. In a way I felt I owed him another try for what he had done for me. And I did love him, even thought I knew he wasn't good for me. The lifestyle was a big hook, I will admit. On and off I really trusted him that we would get married.

"I got so depressed at one point that I had to go on medication. It felt like I was in a black hole. I planned to leave and tried to save some money first. My attitude was, 'You are just a bastard, and now I'm here to use you.' I got a job, and it scared him to death. He swore he would marry me if I quit my job. I did, but we didn't marry. Instead he booted me out of the house without my belongings.

"I had thought about suicide, but a girlfriend let me stay with her. It took me a while to realize Seth couldn't hurt me. Yet when I went to get my clothes and the manager of his apartment house wouldn't let me in, I became enraged. When Seth finally showed up, I threw things and broke a glass table and mirror.

"Seth keeps calling to try and get me back. It's six months and I'm still out here on my own! I have a job and a small support system now. I am hardened and strong enough that I won't go back. I don't entirely regret all of it. I wouldn't be where I am now if it weren't for Seth. I do feel like I have missed my youth. Observing a girlfriend my age reminds me of how young I really am."

Don't Exchange Love for Debt

What could possibly make pretty, bright young women assume mountains of debt that isn't their own when they move in? Women who did say they:

- perceived this magnanimous gesture as appropriate for live-ins, befitting a couple who shares a pantry
- saw assuming their man's debt as an expression of their unwavering love
- thought that straightening out his bungled finances would hurry them on their road to matrimony.

What these women failed to see is that accepting any responsibility, even for his smallest debt, is involving oneself in very risky business. Becoming entwined in each other's financial woes may prevent the easy escape one might seek down the road.

Alice, Co-signed with Regret

"Yes. I'm a pushover," admits Alice, a soft-spoken, self-supporting, young blond in her early twenties. "I always gave David too much of myself. He is used to taking instead of giving. At one point we were going to get married, but I gave him back the ring. He couldn't even buy me a dollar card for Valentine's Day. I co-signed for his car loan and am trying to get him to refinance it. I want my name off the debt. He won't talk about it. I am moving out in a few months and am worried that this won't be resolved."

Hannah Reduced His Debt by Half

Hannah has a tremendous investment in her relationship with Ronnie. When she moved in three years ago, it was supposed to be on a temporary basis. She needed a place to stay while she struck out on her own. Before long, there was talk of love and a lifetime for two. That's when Hannah decided she better get Ronnie's affairs in order. Frivolous, fiscally irresponsible, and $40,000 in debt, Ronnie didn't seem to wince at Hannah's management and the pooling of their resources.

Today, Hannah has reduced his debt to $20,000, is still not engaged, and admits she would have money in the bank if she lived on her own. Nonetheless, this industrious young woman maintains that once the remainder of *their* debt is paid off and Ronnie has money for a down payment on a house and the cash for a ring, he will be willing to walk the road to matrimony.

That's a large investment to walk away from before the interest comes due. The question remains: What is Ronnie's payment plan? There is little evidence he has budgeted for that yet. His agenda calls for erasing all debt and *then* talking marriage. He argues that he wouldn't want Hannah responsible for the $20,000 if they married and something should happen to him. Curiously, though, while she is helping to reduce the debt, her investment continues to mount with Ronnie's latest job transfer to another city, where he expects her to follow, forfeiting job and friends.

Nancy Printed Her Name on the Dotted Line

Nancy, another responsible money manager and live-in partner, started off her interview asking me a question: "Do you think it is normal to get cold feet a few months before your wedding?"

I answered with my own question. "Have you discussed this with your fiance? Have you suggested waiting a little longer to marry?"

"I did bring it up," she admitted, "but with little success. Frank took it the wrong way. He said if I wasn't sure, we should just call it off permanently and that he would move out."

Before I could ask what was wrong with that, she gave me the answer. She had assumed all of Frank's debt by consolidating it under one loan. Her name was on the dotted line.

Don't Let the Heart Take Over

This isn't a story about a woman who loves too much. It is a story about a woman who loved *unwisely*.

I first contacted Julie four months after George had walked out. As soon as I introduced myself over the phone and explained that I was calling to see if she would share her experiences with me for a book, she began to cry.

"I can't talk about it yet," she told me, but she said that I was welcome to try her again in a few months. Seven months after George vacated Julie's lovely home, we met in her kitchen. She cried nonstop for three hours as she told me her story.

"There are some women who can open themselves to a man, to love, and when it's over, it's over. That's never been me," she began. "I know happiness is a real option, just as sorrow is. I always choose happiness because that is my personality, but I haven't been able to lately. I want to get back to being happy. Some people say loving like this is worth the experience. I don't know if I agree. It is too painful. And living together made it worse."

Julie—in her mid-forties, divorced for over fifteen years, good-looking, fun-loving, self-sufficient, intelligent, and sociable—fell madly for George. "I loved him the first time I saw him," Julie admits. "He was the man of my dreams. I always dated a lot, but none of my other relationships felt this way. I thought finally my single life would come to an end. I lost control in this relationship because I loved him so much. I wish he had told me that I was losing control of myself."

George, however, may not have been ready for love. He had recently separated from his wife of twenty-two years after a long period of unhappiness and had had little time to sample single life and date around. Within weeks of meeting, Julie and George began dating exclusively.

A year later when George's lease was up on on his $1,000-a-month apartment, which the couple used only on weekends, it seemed reasonable for him to move into Julie's home, where they already spent Sunday through Thursday. Taking only a few knick-knacks to Julie's, he divided his household possessions between a storage unit and his mother's house, where he conducted his weekend visitations with his children.

"We both enjoyed playing house. We always cooked together, and on Saturday evenings we were content to sit curled up together in front of a fire and not go out. I felt secure just having him there, with his pictures hanging on the walls. It was enough for the moment. I didn't expect more at the time."

Julie felt lucky. "George was a real catch. He is a decent human being, well educated, and from an upper-middle-class family. I knew there would be a line waiting for him if he weren't dating me at the time," she says. "Good men are hard to find. Really neat single women are plentiful."

Despite the apparent seriousness of the relationship and Julie's intent to become George's wife, she never seriously brought up the subject of matrimony before or after George moved in. She was waiting for his divorce to become final. In the meantime, her mission was to make George's life in her home comfy, cozy, and trouble-free.

"He was having serious financial problems, and the banks were recalling loans on his investments right and left. His divorce was messy and proceeding slowly, and the kids weren't coming through it all that well. I tried to make it all better. I created a protective environment for him," Julie explains. "I didn't want to pressure him about marriage. I wanted him to forget the outside world when he came home. I kept telling him not to worry about what he lost, that we would have each other and there would always be a roof over our heads.

"I thought I was everything he wanted, because I was everything his wife wasn't. I thought the motions we were going through living together were toward a lifetime together. But in retrospect, I see now that he was going through the motions of being comfortable. I had a stable life, so I could make his life easier. He needed me because of the things that were missing in his life and the problems he was having. In the beginning he couldn't be without me. I mistook his need for love," she says.

"I didn't face the real issues. I didn't want to see them. Don't make the mistake of putting on blinders," warns Julie. "I failed to look at anything that indicated things might not be just fine. I still probably don't see the complete truth, and I won't until the wound is healed."

Julie closed her eyes to George's intentions, assuming they were akin to her own, and misinterpreted his language to suit her idyllic notions. Here are some of the signs Julie said should have tipped her off that things were awry:

1. "George never said, 'I want to marry you,' and he never said, 'I am *in love* with you,'" Julie explains. "He did say, 'I don't know how to love. I can't love like you. I don't know if I am in love with you. I can't love you as much as you love me. It isn't you; it's me.'"

What she thought he was saying to her was more like, "I haven't had experience in a good loving relationship because I didn't love my wife and I don't relate well to my family. It will take me time to learn how to love. I know if I could love, I would be in love with you."

Julie found out later what he was really trying to say: "I do not love you, Julie." What she has come to regret was not asking him why he didn't and if he ever would.

2. Julie realizes she failed to recognize signs of trouble and to act when George's divorce became final. They had dated for two years by then and had been roommates for more than six months. George was restless. He would be up early sitting in the kitchen, distracted and deep in thought.

"I just figured he was worried about the banks and his financial problems. I didn't ask him if it had anything to do with our relationship," Julie says. "About the same time, he told me he wanted to get his own apartment, that his kids were growing away from him. He ended up moving out two months later.

"A good friend of both of ours had tried to warn me, I think, several months before we broke up. The three of us were at the warehouse where George had stored his things. I saw this wonderful lamp and told him I would like to take it home where we could both use it. My friend told me later she saw fear on his face.

"My thought was, 'How silly that is. He knows if he wants the lamp back, he can have it.' I should have been more open to her comment, and I should have asked him if he was afraid of anything. It is obvious now he was having some serious doubts about our relationship."

3. This is the toughest blind spot; maybe it's the part Julie says she can't entirely face until her wound is healed. It has to do with how Julie and George parted, why they parted, and what has happened to George since they parted. Perhaps you will see some of the signs that Julie didn't.

A few months before George announced he "needed to be single and experience single life," Julie and he were at a large late-night outdoor function. Carol, an attractive woman in her late thirties, just happened to wander into their little group, complaining that she had become separated from her friends and was stranded. Being the caring, empathizing person Julie is, she invited this woman to join them, indicating that they would take her home shortly.

In less than two months George moved out, and this very woman became a visible part of his life one week later. Carol became pregnant. Julie is certain that George was not having an affair while they were still living together but that he might have looked Carol up at work during that time. Carol had told George and Julie that she was a retail clerk where George happened to shop now and then. Whatever the sequence of events, however he really met her, or whenever they became lovers, the fact is that within weeks this woman became George's new housemate and is almost certain to become his new wife after their child is born.

One thing Julie will admit: *"When you get your eyesight back, it hurts like hell!"*

Don't Forget Where You're Headed

No matter how astute or aggressive a woman may be in the workplace, if she doesn't use those same skills to manage her live-in relationship and keep sight of her personal goals, she may find herself heading in the wrong direction.

Taking a Detour

"It takes a lot of willpower *not* to move in with your boy-friend," concedes Beth, who wishes she had used the same clear decision making that she is professionally known for in planning national advertising strategy.

At twenty-five years of age, Beth started dating Stan, who was two years older. They found one another fun and intellectually stimulating. Around the same time, Beth had just purchased a home that needed repair and decorating. She and Stan spent many hours working together over buckets of paint and rolls of wallpaper.

"With both of us putting so much time into the house, it seemed very natural to have Stan move in with me when the house was ready. I loved him and thought we were headed for marriage," says Beth.

"Not long after I began sharing my home," she continues, "I received the job offer of a lifetime, but it would require me to work out of state. I thought I could take the job and Stan, a teacher employed nine months out of the year, could come up for the summer. That way we wouldn't have to be away from each other as much. He did not want me to move, and he would not go away with me. He refused to live farther than a three-hour drive from his parents' home. He felt they needed him. He talked about how much he loved me and how afraid he was that if I went, I wouldn't come back. Basically, he gave me an ultimatum: If you go, it's over. It was very emotional.

"I didn't want to give Stan up. It was a hard decision," Beth admits. "If we hadn't been living together, I would have taken the job, but I didn't feel like I was in a very secure position to fight for my side. If we were married, I would have felt I had more leverage and could have fought harder and more safely for my point of view.

"Things went downhill after that," recalls Beth. "I guess there are some regrets. I felt like I was at a standstill for a whole year. I had a miserable time working in a position locally that was not paying much and was boring and mundane. I was feeling so worthless that my opinion of myself suffered. I had always been a good worker, and what I did for a living was very important to me. I became emotionally and financially dependent upon Stan at that time. It would have been more tolerable if at least my relationship with him was moving forward. He didn't want to become engaged because he said we might be doing it for the wrong reasons, namely to distract me from my unhappiness at my job or to give me something exiting to do.

"I knew I had to make some changes, but I wanted to go in a direction that Stan would approve of. I decided to apply to graduate school. With my credentials, I think I could have gotten into some of the more prestigious business schools out of state. But Stan clearly did not want me leaving, so I applied to the local university. To do otherwise would have made me feel like the selfish, independent bitch Stan implied I acted like.

"It wasn't until several months later, when out of necessity I temporarily accepted a job two hours away and spent Monday through Friday at a friend's, that I began to have some second thoughts about our relationship. I woke up one morning and didn't know myself. The separation helped me to see that I was doing things that I didn't want to do," concludes Beth.

"Empowered with the success at my job and being out of the house enabled me to step back and look at our relationship objectively. I was putting Stan's agenda ahead of mine. It made me realize that he was the one that was being too uncompromising. I felt that I was giving up all of my dreams and fulfilling *his* ideal life. He was forcing me to make more concessions than I was really comfortable with."

After Beth returned from a three-week European trip with her mother, during which she did not speak to Stan, several additional events jolted her senses. "When I got home, I told Stan that I would have to cancel out on a summer trip we had planned. I needed to use all of the money I had saved for grad school. He had no respect for what I was going through and was furious over my backing out. I don't know why I didn't realize before that he was so selfish. It hurt me, because in many other ways I had tried so hard to be giving to him.

"I told him then that not only could I not travel with him that summer, but I thought we needed to end our relationship and he needed to move out," Beth says with authority. "It probably would have happened sooner if I hadn't had to ask him to leave and I could have been the one to walk out of his home. It was traumatic for him, but it wasn't for me because I knew that I was doing the right thing. I had felt trapped. Now all of a sudden, all of my options were available to me again.

"I know now," emphasizes Beth, "that it *is* possible to have a professional life and a healthy relationship at the same time. I didn't know that then. I don't think I could have had that with Stan. I don't plan to live with anyone again until I marry and I feel certain I can be myself."

Never Sell Yourself Short

Stephanie's story is a three-year nightmare she would like to forget. Sitting across a table from this articulate, controlled, motivated, and focused young woman, it is hard to believe that five years ago she fell so deeply into a dangerous abyss.

Stephanie's Fragile State of Mind

Stephanie was raised in a protected upper-middle-class environment. She cast aside many of the values of her suburban family when she entered her first live-in relationship at age twenty. Six years later, Craig was to become Stephanie's third live-in lover and, she says adamantly, "my last."

"It was one of those relationships that belongs on Oprah," she begins. "He was so charming and attractive. I thought, 'Wow. I can't believe this incredible-looking guy likes me.' I would have gone to any lengths at the time to make sure we were together. I thought having him move in put me in control. By supporting him, I could manipulate him into needing me and staying. I paid for absolutely everything and rationalized, 'Why not? I would be paying rent and utilities anyway.' I wanted to get married, but I knew it wasn't even an option with him. I am sure he had no intention of marrying me.

"Craig worked on my self-esteem and would say things that made me feel so bad," Stephanie reveals. "He said I was crazy. I began to question my own self-worth and sanity. He controlled me by manipulating the way I thought about myself. Craig knew that I needed and wanted sex and attention. Consequently he was loving and comforting to me when I got very angry with him and he thought I might throw him out. Generally, however, he withheld sex entirely from me and made me feel that no one else would want me. He would not respond to my advances, which cut me to the bone. That made me question my sexuality and what it was about me that made him not want to have sex. I thought I couldn't possibly be attractive to other men.

"He was entirely different in public. He made sure to give our family and friends the right impression," Stephanie continues. "He charmed by parents totally. They really liked him and knew very little about our relationship. In front of others, he would hug and kiss me and call me 'Honey.' People thought we were the perfect couple.

"The whole thing got really ugly. I still can't believe I allowed this to happen. It was a very violent relationship with yelling, screaming, and hitting. When I think of it, I think, 'Oh God. I can't even believe it was me.' He pushed me down one night, bruising me all over and knocking out several teeth. I had to be taken to the hospital. When he threatened to kill me, I called my parents. I had to get a restraining order to protect myself. If he came near my house, the police would arrest him.

"I remember sitting in the prosecutor's office when the clerk told me I was the sixth or seventh woman who had filed a domestic violence complaint against Craig. My neighbors called one night and said they thought he was living in my basement. The police came and took him away. All night I thought about this poor guy in jail.

"I was kidding myself about the whole relationship. It has taken several years to build back my self-esteem."

RED WARNING SIGNS

April, Stephanie, and all the women in this chapter failed to recognize signs that signaled trouble. To avoid their mishaps:

1. Determine if any of the symptoms applied to women at risk apply to you.

2. Ask yourself if your relationship looks like risky business.

3. Be aware of your own frailties and insecurities.

4. Pay attention when you are unhappy and ask why.

5. Be cautious of men who are:
   • down on their luck
   • controlling
   • failing to reciprocate your love or respect
   • inexperienced in love
   • recently divorced or separated from a spouse or lover
   • unwilling to contribute equally emotionally or financially
   • limiting your horizons.

CHAPTER 3

Hazards for Men

Men are not immune to the hazards of live-in love. They get their pockets picked and their hearts broken. Female partners may not deliberately set out to wreak havoc on their men's lives, but they sometimes do because some men are:

- in denial
- full of guilt
- protective of their "macho" image.

Frequently, men who find live-in love a mistake compromise their happiness and well-being long before they realize they have given away more than their hearts.

CAUTION SIGNS FOR MEN

Men who are likely to have problems moving in may be identified by one or more of the following characteristics:

- poor judges of women
- lonely
- romantic
- impulsive

+ gullible
+ inexperienced in love
+ nurturers and caretakers
+ uncomfortable with confrontation
+ ruled by male ego
+ easily manipulated by women.

These are the men who all too often get their lives spun upside down when the wheel of live-in love starts turning. They are particularly vulnerable if they happen to be:

+ re-entering single life
+ on the rebound
+ in love and in lust
+ unable to live alone
+ suffering a money pinch.

If you are a man who falls into this group, *watch out!*

WOMEN WHO MAY GET YOU HAD

Indeed there are women who intend to take full advantage of the unassuming male victim. They are, however, much less common than the typical female who inadvertently ends up getting her man had. Both kinds of women share these characteristics:

+ lack of ability to be independent
+ financial insecurity
+ inexperienced living on her own
+ a variety of personal problems
+ inadequate maturity and personal growth.

YOU'RE ABOUT TO BE HAD

Men appear to have a particularly difficult time reading the signs that their live-in relationships are heading downhill. And in all fairness to these men, these signals are sometimes purposely vague, well camouflaged, and difficult to decipher. The most obvious signals are abrupt changes in the woman's attitude toward and interaction with her live-in lover. These include behaviors such as:

- a marked decline in sexual activity
- an argumentative demeanor
- a desire to spend more time alone
- a withdrawal from the relationship
- a genre of phrases repeatedly used by women who are gearing up to pull out.

The big tip-offs for these salutations are their overly considerate, excessively solicitous, and self-defacing language.

Example. "You have to experience life on your own. It would be better for the relationship if we lived apart," is typical of these send-offs. Twenty-four-year-old Kimberly states she could not believe her live-in beau of one year actually believed this line, designed to speed his exit. Why the sudden urgency for him to pack his bags? "I was hanging onto him because there was no one else, and I had this big house. I just didn't want him there after I met Ted."

Example. Some women may revise the focus of Kimberly's excuse, but the real message is the same: "I need to know what it is like to be on my own." Those who utter this one mean, "I am no longer interested in living with you."

Example. "I'm really not good enough for you," is an ego boosting line for sure. It is repeated frequently by partners in the waning days of live-in relationships as a ploy to gently dissolve the partnership.

MEN WHO GOT HAD

Four categories of these men prominently emerge from my series of interviews. They get caught by a runaway "mutual use," failure to objectively examine their prospective partner, the pleasure of rescuing their lady love, or young women who are not ready to hand over their hearts. Their mishaps have striking resemblances even though the particulars vary.

A "Mutual Use" Out of Control

Mutual users risk losing control of their destiny. Kevin is a prime example. He willingly agreed to candidly share his dilemma, revealing his pain, frustration, and difficulty in saying good-bye to his live-in lady.

Committing without Being Committed

Kevin was twenty-four when he met twenty-three-year-old Rosemary at work. "What attracted me to her originally was sex. At the beginning there was an eagerness to do whatever I suggested. Consequently, Rosemary stayed over 90 percent of the time. I don't think I ever consented to her moving in. It just happened. I really didn't want it from the get-go, but I felt kind of responsible for her," admits Kevin.

"She had only been in town a few months when I hooked her up to room with a couple of girls I knew. She didn't get along well with them and wanted to move out. We had been dating for a year by then and her parents felt more comfortable having her live with me than alone. That added to my sense of responsibility for her."

Kevin does concede that while he went into the arrangement partially blinded, he did see some personal advantages to it. "I was tired of running around and leading a single's lifestyle. I liked the idea of having a companion at home whom I could bounce things off, and I thought it would make things easier financially. I was struggling to meet payments on my new house and college loans. When Rosemary moved in, she paid for some of the incidentals and the food. I also felt like I was under a lot of pressure from my buddies who were getting married to do the same. To my way of thinking I was postponing making that kind of commitment by having Rosemary move in with me."

According to Kevin, the first year was actually pretty good

and, from all indications, an even exchange. "I was fixing her situation, and at the same time she was giving order to my life, establishing boundaries and guidelines. She is very thrifty, and I am a real spendthrift. For a period that first year, there was a time I even thought I really wanted to get married. I went so far as to look for rings."

Announcements from his brother and a close friend that each was headed for a divorce started Kevin thinking. "I wasn't sure why I was getting married and if Rosemary loved me or the idea of getting married. I didn't want to settle for something that was sub-par," Kevin explains. "I wanted to do the right thing. Two things I feel the strongest about are marriage and raising kids."

Rosemary was comfortable living in Kevin's home, but he began having serious doubts, which he failed to communicate. The relationship underwent a tremendous shift at the beginning of the second year of living together.

"I realized that I loved Rosemary as a person and I cared about her well-being, but I didn't love her as I would a wife for the rest of my life," he says, still pained by his revelations. "I began to see a lot of things about her I couldn't live with. She was too bitchy, too negative, and too dependent. Our whole relationship just seemed to fizzle. Sex was practically nonexistent. She complained that it was painful to have intercourse and begged off most of the time. Her doctor could not find anything wrong and suggested she read some books on sex. I started feeling bitter and angry toward her after being rejected so often.

"I still thought I could work it out," says Kevin remorsefully, "but I knew that I wouldn't be able to honor my commitment to marry Rosemary. When I came to this conclusion I felt relieved in my own mind. I should have left right away, but I wasn't ready for it to be over, either. I was weak and didn't tell her how I was feeling. She started calling me a liar and throwing it up to me because we weren't getting married."

Kevin's regret grew steadily, but still he preferred to suffer in silence rather than confront Rosemary. "I felt like I was missing out on things and started steaming inside with resentment. I kept mulling over in my mind how I could end the relationship. I wished she would just go away."

At about this time, suddenly Kevin's career took off and he was able to foot most of the bills. Meanwhile, Rosemary went back to school to become a paralegal, which Kevin hoped would make her independent and provide him with the possibility of escape.

"I definitely felt trapped, but I couldn't just boot Rosemary out of my house. I wanted her to save as much money as she could so that way when she graduated from school she would be able to make it on her own," says Kevin, the classic middle-child crowd pleaser. "I felt obligated to wait until she could be independent. I had made the wrong decision to have her move in and I had to deal with the consequences. I wanted to handle this smoothly, waiting for the right opportunity to present itself."

Now a year later, Kevin is still awaiting the proper moment to broach the subject of splitting up. It seems Rosemary did not graduate on time due to her mother's illness, which compelled her to drop out a semester. "I have not been able to get on with my life," complains Kevin, who disclosed during our recent conversation that he wants to begin looking for a more suitable marriage partner.

"I think Rosemary still has hopes we will get engaged. I don't understand why she would want to marry me. Our relationship is so bad. I have very little respect left for her because I think she would say yes in a flash. I was monogamous and did not date other women until this year, when my job started taking me out of town. I hope I will be free in another month, but I am worried it won't end easily.

"I will be hurt, and I am scared knowing that she will be, too. I feel like I am the bad guy, but I don't really believe that is all true. It would be different if it weren't my house. I could walk out. I know that no matter what I say or how I say it, breaking the news won't be pleasant. I have to come to grips with the fact that I won't win either way. I won't be a nice guy. If I have to sell the house to move her out, I will. I feel that so much time has passed that I have paid my debt to her already. You bet I've been had," he says for the first time emphatically.

◆　◆　◆

Failing to Look before Crossing the Threshold of Live-In Love

A number of men, intensely feeling the need to have a woman around, act impulsively and fail to take a good hard look at the females they invite to share their breakfast tables. Consequently, they make careless and costly mistakes. One man with whom I talked, Lucas, had troubles that were outrageous enough to qualify for the juiciest television soap operas.

Trouble Enough for a Midday Soap

Poor Lucas, thirty-five years old, suffered through his real-life drama. He is lovable, hardworking, generous—a good catch, but unlucky at love. Quickly falling in love and in *lust* over any number of females who expertly massage his ego and his libido, he admittedly rarely takes time to find out if a woman spells trouble.

"I'm a pushover when it comes to women, because I enjoy them and would rather spend time with a woman than with the guys," he explains. "I get great enjoyment out of buying women presents and saying, 'Here, honey, I love you.'"

Lucas experienced a shotgun wedding early in his college years and tried unsuccessfully to complete his degree while supporting his wife and two children. Two years after his subsequent divorce he began his first live-in affair. It was full of passion and conflict.

"She wanted me to do all of the bending," is Lucas's assessment. "She wanted more time and attention than I could give. Maybe it was selfish, but I wanted to devote time to my career and I needed the weekends to study. I was determined to succeed this time and get my degree. She also wanted children and I had previously had a vasectomy. It could be reversed, I suppose, but I really didn't want any more children. We argued so much that we went to counseling. Gail just wouldn't give in on anything. She was so hardheaded. Our counselor even told her that there were a million girls who would love to be in her shoes."

That didn't seem to matter to Gail. When the relationship ended after three years, Lucas was stricken with grief. "She wanted to date other guys and said she wasn't sure if she wanted to spend the rest of her life with me. After she left, I would come home and walk into her closets. I could still smell her perfume, and I missed her badly. Nobody wants to be alone."

And alone he was until Nancy, a young unwed mother in her early twenties, engineered his latest fiasco and moved in ninety days after her predecessor vacated the premises.

Nancy and Lucas had been friends for several years, becoming acquainted during Lucas's frequent business trips to Iowa. He assumed the role of confidant and big brother during the ordeal of her pregnancy and delivery, which coincided with his lover's departure. Nancy and Lucas's platonic relationship took a sharp and immediate right turn onto a sexual, passionate, and romantic road a few months before Gail made her move. It wasn't hard for Nancy to convince Lucas in her love letters that she wanted to be with him and that dating long-distance would inhibit the growth of their relationship.

"Without a doubt, it was stupid," says Lucas with hindsight. "She wanted to come to Philadelphia to date and to get to know me better. There was no other way we could do that unless she moved in." That's how baby and Nancy came to move into Lucas's large, luxurious home. And that's how Lucas has come to be a generous, loving surrogate daddy who paid most of the bills, showering both mother and daughter with $40,000 worth of travel, gifts, and household freebies.

Lucas's life at home was more settled than on the road. Nancy wanted to play. "She thinks I am a horse's ass because I study and can't party with her," says Lucas. It has not been unusual, therefore, for Lucas to pick Nancy's baby up at the sitter's on a Friday evening, feed and bathe her, read a bedtime story, and then finally hit his books thoroughly exhausted. Lucas chalks Nancy's behavior up to immaturity but is noticeably unhappy over her behavior and how things are working out.

For starters he is not pleased about her bar hopping with friends one or two nights a week. If she comes in past midnight, then she is ready for bed at eight the next evening. "Coming home late is not an excuse to avoid intimacy. We have a good sex life," he says defensively, "but we don't have much time together, and that really pisses me off."

"It's not that I think she is having an affair or anything. I know where she is at all times and who she is with when she goes to the bars. And if she goes back to the office once or twice a week at night to complete some of her secretarial responsibilities, she always calls to let me know she is on her way home so that I won't worry. To make this relationship work, I have told her she will have to start putting me and the baby ahead of her friends and stop playing around."

Lucas knows he isn't perfect, either, but insists Nancy will have to grow up if they are going to get married. Why is Lucas waiting to see if Nancy can or will change? "I don't want to fail again," he answers. "I'm tired of it. I am successful at my work. I don't know why I can't be successful at love. I'm tired. I'm thirty-five. I miss growing up with my kids, and I like having Nancy's child around. I'm at the point where I'm questioning what I'm doing wrong. I'll be the loser in this one because I won't be getting what I want. At first she talked about marriage. Now she has stopped mentioning it. *She tells me that I deserve someone better than her.*"

Nancy persuaded Lucas it was indeed time for her to pack up after this stint, which lasted just under two years. And Lucas, feeling guilty for partaking in this mutual pursuit and allowing her to move so far from home, doubting he ever loved her, has chosen to give her a generous send-off. He will help pay off her credit cards, provide deposits for her apartment furniture, give her the baby's furniture, and clean the slate on her car repairs and tires.

"I am a little angry and bitter. I put two years into this and thought we would settle down. I don't want to be here when she moves out. It will be very hard," he acknowledges, his voice cracking.

A year later, I checked in with Lucas. Nancy is gone, but Lucas, although a trifle more careful in his relationships, is still trusting questionably. He told me that after he and Nancy broke up, they did not continue dating as he imagined they would. Rather, she immediately and openly began an affair with a mutual friend who had regularly traveled and socialized with them with his now-estranged wife.

"I did ask Nancy if she was seeing this guy while she was still living with me," he reveals. "She said no. I think she is telling the truth."

Do you?

The Knight-in-Shining-Armor Syndrome

This syndrome is problematic for the knight and the damsel in distress. The damsel will tell you that she suffered at his hands. The knight will tell you she took advantage of his chivalry. Whether it is the man or the woman who gets had is not always clear. Both have something to lose. What is abundantly clear is that neither plans to give anything away for free.

The conflict begins as soon as a woman entrusts herself into a man's keeping and he is emotionally gratified by becoming her keeper. As one man succinctly put it, "I like being the big kahoona." This may be well and good for the moment, but it leaves the man wide open to be had—before and after marriage.

Kerianne and Helen are the damsels whose stories we will next explore.

Questionable Motives on the Damsel's Side

Kerianne was just nineteen when her cozy world fell apart. She was off enjoying her freshman year at an expensive private university when she found out that her father had suffered a major financial reversal and that funds for the next school year were not forthcoming. Consciously or unconsciously, she set out to remedy her situation. Through happenstance she met Mark, seven years older and already reasonably well-established.

"I thought he was put in my life for a reason. I was so emotionally needy at that time, and he encouraged and supported me," begins this dark-eyed, dark-haired, vivacious beauty. "He wanted to take all of my pain away and do everything for me. When my mother said I had to come home in three months, I moved in with Mark. I thought it was going to be temporary, but I was really captivated by him and believed I was in love. I was in love with the things we did, not with him. He had all of the material things I envisioned having myself."

Helen, like Kerianne, admits that a man came to her rescue. Today a visibly self-assured woman in her mid-forties, Helen at twenty-four was recovering from a verbally and emotionally abusive relationship when she completed her graduate studies and became reacquainted with Sam, an old friend from her undergrad days. To protect herself, she formulated a practical mental image of the kind of man she wanted to establish a permanent relationship with. Sam was it: on the rise, extremely intelligent, a friend first and passion last.

"He was supposedly in love with me," Helen explains, although today she wonders if he understood what that meant. As for herself, she is perfectly honest: "I had made a conscious choice to make him my partner. I had hoped to learn to love him."

When Helen moved to Atlanta knowing no one except Sam, she accepted his invitation to share his apartment. "I was scared to be independent. I was sort of coming out of my parents' nest and out of school at the same time. It was scary having to think of taking care of myself," Helen says, admitting she isn't making her youthful self sound very noble. "Going into a safe relationship where there wasn't a whole lot of emotional investment—plus the benefits of a beautiful apartment in an expensive large city—seemed perfect."

Both of these women paid a high price for these gallant knights with seemingly good intentions.

Kerianne continues her saga. "Mark was loving but also very condescending and treated me like a child. I really wanted to live on my own, but I didn't think I could. He just kind of pushed himself on me. We became engaged after four months, and after six months my self-esteem began to diminish. I felt like a non-person. I didn't have to do anything. I didn't have to go to school or to work. In fact, he encouraged me to stay home. He liked to keep me under his finger and liked me to need him. He refused to notice when I was becoming an alcoholic and instead encouraged me to drink because sex was better when I did.

"I tried to call off the wedding and went home to talk to my parents. They said I was just experiencing the normal premarital jitters. They were dead wrong. I couldn't wait for him to go out of town on business just to have a breathing spell. I knew I had to get out of this relationship and realized I never would have married him if we hadn't moved in together."

Helen came to that same conclusion, even though she and Sam lived together for two years before marrying. She was the one who pressed the marriage issue, tired of being treated by his business associates as "the concubine." But from the time Helen entrusted herself to him, Sam was the one who called most of the shots.

"We were doing fairly well together in the beginning," Helen recounts. "I was working and making a decent salary, but still I was financially and emotionally dependent upon Sam. In a lot of ways he was my mentor. He wasn't domineering, but he was smothering. He wanted someone to love him so completely that I could never think of another man. He wanted us to be bonded at the hip. I had trouble with that because I didn't go into the relationship nuts about him. Because of this, our sex life was less than terrific. I wasn't really physically attracted to Sam and blamed my lack of interest frequently on medical problems.

"He was transferred to Chicago, and we thought it best if I stay in Atlanta, since he anticipated moving back in one year. He subsidized my salary by sending me one or two hundred dollars a month. Meantime, I am not a person who likes being alone. I started seeing another man and went away with him on a weekend.

"Sam tried to reach me that whole weekend. When he finally did, I told him where I had been. The next day he flew to Atlanta and told me to pack my bags—I was moving to Chicago. It was almost like my father telling me what to do. I wasn't ready to end the relationship, so I went. I don't entirely understand why, other than I was so dependent and needed him for security. I was afraid I would never find anyone else who would provide for me as well financially and be my friend.

"We got married about a year later, when Sam had to make another career move to St. Louis. We moved together, but it was devastating for my career. Through his business contacts Sam got me assigned to a great temporary project in Chicago. Being on my own enabled me to grow in my own direction rather than constantly undergoing Sam's scrutiny and his attempts to mold me into his own likeness, which went against my natural grain."

What did it take for both of these distressed damsels to leave their knights with tarnished armor?

"I started back to school in about a year," Kerianne says. "Mark paid for school, but I got a part-time job because I felt like I was using him. I was having an affair, and all along I was wondering when I could make my break. Mark knew I was unhappy and recommended we seek marriage counseling. Every time the counselor asked me a question, he answered it for me. After one session, the counselor told me that I should get out of the marriage; she knew I was miserable having him control my life.

"I went to work and got two jobs. I knew nothing about money. I have never even balanced a checkbook. He picked me up from work one day, and on the way out to dinner I told him that I couldn't stay married to him. He stopped the car in the middle of the expressway, hollering and crying. It was a nightmare. I wanted to leave right away, but I agreed to wait a week. It was the longest week of my life. I even considered suicide, because I knew I had hurt him so terribly. I thought if I didn't exist any longer, it would solve a lot of problems. I finally moved home and told my parents I needed help."

Helen's exit was not as dramatic, but it certainly was as liberating for her and as painful for her husband. While in Chicago enjoying the stimulation of her job, she met Tim, who eventually became her lover and has been her husband for the past twelve years.

"When we started going out, it was in a group after work," Helen explains. "Then when the two of us started seeing each other alone, there were no strings attached; I never thought I was going to end up leaving Sam for Tim. But when the job was over and I went back home, Sam and I had a tremendous fight. I don't even remember now what it was about. I realized, however, that the intimate relationship I had been developing with Tim gave me a great deal of strength. Like a number of women, I needed another relationship to break out of the one I was in. Sam was extremely bitter. He had absolutely no idea of what had gone wrong and probably doesn't to this day. I was never really honest with him about why I went into the relationship in the first place."

Anything less than an exchange of honesty indicates that surely someone will be had in live-in love.

Love 'Em and Leave 'Em

We have already encountered a number of women who cheated on their live-in lovers—even after they became their husbands. It is obvious that infidelity can occur at any age, and perpetrators are not restricted to one gender. This discovery is nonetheless a particularly painful awakening for men. They see it as the "ultimate betrayal," the most devastating form of rejection. Infidelity by one's lover cuts to the core of their male being and chisels away at their ego. The pain is greatly magnified for the young, idealistic, trusting man who out of love has committed to a monogamous live-in relationship that he thinks is heading toward a lifetime together.

Tom, a young man I was referred to, lived with his wife for five years before they were married. Six months after tying the knot, Tom found her sleeping with another man. Evidently he thought I might be calling to chastise him for his poor lack of foresight, as his family and friends had been doing.

"Ask my friends," he suggested politely but with a chill. "They know all the details. I just don't want to hear about it again."

Romance on the College Campus

There were enough cases among college coeds in which the live-in male partner was had to warrant a note of caution. It is not surprising that so many of these relationships do not form long-lasting partnerships. Some studies show that the initial incentives for coeds to cohabit are based upon more superficial aspects of a relationship such as convenience, economics, security, and companionship. Nonetheless, the discovery of a live-in partner's indiscretion is still painful.

Cindy and Hal, a typical example, were both in college when their romance began. Nightly encounters got to be a habit and led to a more convenient live-in relationship. Three months later, Hal, three years older than his lady, pledged his undying love and asked Cindy to marry him. The couple became engaged but declined to name a date for the wedding, just saying it was to take place in the distant future.

The distant future never arrived for this couple.

"Once I graduated and started working different hours, we hardly saw one another. I think we grew apart," says Hal.

"I thought she was spending most of her time at the library," Hal continues. "Cindy was a very good and serious student. I never questioned her if there was anyone else until I found a man's watch in the apartment and a friend of hers told me she was tired of seeing me get messed around. Cindy had been sleeping with another guy for two months, and I failed to see all of the signs I know now were there."

They were the classic ones: Cindy became less affectionate, less interested in sex, less interested in spending time with Hal, and much more argumentative.

"I think I subconsciously knew something was going on, but I ignored it. There was a lot of security and safety in having this relationship. My only other semi-serious girlfriend was one from high school. I had no choice but to confront Cindy after I found the watch and her friend squealed. She admitted it right away. I walked out and haven't talked to her in four years. It was very traumatic for me. It still hurts, and I still care about her," he admits.

Looking back gives Hal a good perspective on what happened to his love affair. "I think we smothered each other. There was no avenue for growth during a period in our lives that required it. Our relationship was too consuming. We should have formed a better foundation for our relationship before even thinking of moving in together. I would do it over differently today. We needed to become friends first."

STOP, LOOK, AND LISTEN

These are some of the circumstances that spell trouble. If they describe what is happening to you:

1. Step back and take a good honest look at your relationship.

2. Ask yourself what each of you is getting out of the arrangement.

3. Define her motives.

4. Read between the lines.

5. Ask yourself, "Am I in a situation where I stand a good chance of being had?"

6. If the answer is yes, decide what you are going to do about it and when.

Procrastinating, shoving the obvious under the rug, and failing to face up to the facts only tightens the trap. You may become one of those stuck in the stalemate of live-in love.

CHAPTER 4

The Stalemate of Live-In Love

"A friend of mine and I were talking about a woman of eighty who recently got married," says Janice, a forty-nine-year-old live-in who has been involved with Bradley for more than ten years. "I said I hoped Bradley and I were married by the time I am that old. My friend said, '*And I doubt you will be a moment before.*'"

It sounds as if Janice's friend has become an astute observer of the stalemate of live-in love. Partners who hold out hope for matrimony allow years to roll by while they play a game of cat and mouse.

Both cat and mouse may report some satisfaction from the game, but one of the two invariably and remorsefully reveals the tension, frustration, disappointment, fatigue, and pain behind the chase.

THE OBJECT OF THE GAME

The real object of cat and mouse is to perpetuate a state of intentional limbo that produces a tolerable status quo. Players employ extensive rationalizations and engage in elaborate charades to avoid having to face one or both of the questions they most want answered:

◆   ◆   ◆

1. Is my live-in lover the person I want to spend a lifetime with, and does he or she want to spend a lifetime with me?

2. Do we have the capacity to make each other happy in a life-long marriage?

HOW TO PLAY THE GAME

Here's how you create the stalemate:

1. Avoid disclosing each and every pertinent issue that could create conflict.
2. Avoid confronting each other's ambivalence.
3. Avoid expectations that lead to disappointment.
4. Avoid dealing with the essence of your own doubts.
5. Avoid making a plan to break the limbo.

WHO PLAYS, WHO WINS, AND FOR HOW LONG

Players are of all ages and start out with varying levels of commitment. The stalemate can develop out of the most casual live-in relationship or the most committed. No one is declared winner or loser during the stalemate. But from the explorations of the love relationships that follow, it is not difficult to determine the high cost of playing.

Players forfeit the opportunity to achieve real satisfaction and happiness by setting aside their goals and hiding behind a palatable but not entirely fulfilling level of comfort. Genuine confusion and the fear of suffering pain, loneliness, or the loss of their partner sabotages their attempts to put an end to the limbo.

The following rounds of play demonstrate how the game of cat and mouse works in the lives of live-in lovers. Counting begins once the couple share a home.

Creating a Safe Haven for the Cat and Happiness for the Mouse

Liz has created a safe haven for Hank. He is free from having to move forward in the relationship and making a firm commitment. At the same time, Liz has reduced the risk of confronting his intentions head on.

What does Liz want?

☑ Liz wants Hank.
☑ She wants Hank to live in her house.
☐ She wants to marry Hank.

So far, Liz has checked off the first two items on her list.

Getting Hank to the altar is a little less certain. And pressing the issue could very well compromise her gains. Consequently, Liz has opted to take advantage of their unusual circumstances that prevents either one of them from getting caught for the moment. It is worth examining how this state of limbo has developed over a decade.

Liz's Obsession

"I thought I was a practical person until I became obsessed with Hank," begins Liz, now in her early forties. "We were friends as couples when each of us was living with our spouses in the suburbs. I separated from my husband after discovering his alternate lifestyle. I was already madly in love with Hank by then, and I pursued him. We started having an affair. I admit it was a terrible thing to do. He didn't leave his wife for two years; however, when he did, he said it was because of me. I think he was looking for an excuse. He hadn't been happy for a long time. They each had their extra-marital affairs. When he moved out of his house, I expected he would be mine. I was so hurt when he wasn't."

That was the beginning of more than five years of turmoil for Liz. Hank moved into his own apartment, dated all kinds of women and lied to Liz, making up the most convoluted stories to hide his whereabouts at times. Nothing could stop Liz in her pursuit.

"I tracked him down when he was with other women. He made me so miserable. I am still angry for the way he treated me. If I had a friend or a sister who behaved the way I did, I would tell her she was sick. I was wrong in not putting my foot down and telling him he couldn't date me *and* other women."

Liz's persistence paid off. After eight years of pining away for Hank, he gave up his bachelor pad, said *adieu* to the other women, and moved into her home without promises or pledges for the next round of this love affair.

"It is what I was striving for," Liz says in all honesty. "Having him to myself and in my home these last two years has made my life more complete."

Liz will tell you that Hank is afraid of marriage. She is not about to press the issue. How can Hank be certain of that? Simple: Both Liz and Hank are still married. Liz's husband has hung on to the formal title of husband and father of their two teenage children as a cover for his homosexual lifestyle for the past twelve years. Hank's wife has held on for the money for the last ten. When Liz does bring up the idea of becoming Hank's wife, he tells her to get her divorce and then he'll get his. So far Liz has not been eager to call his bluff and upset the delicate balance, using the excuse that divorcing her husband could provoke money problems and spark nasty fights.

"I suppose it could go on forever this way," acknowledges Liz.

Why not? Hank has established a perfect level of comfort for himself, although Liz's husband has put a stop to some of her generosity. "My husband was angry because Hank wasn't helping to pay the mortgage or utilities. He said no one should live rent-free. In my heart of hearts, I knew he was right. It's just that I felt so badly for Hank. He had so many expenses with alimony and kids in college. He did do some work on the house, and he paid for some landscaping. He is contributing more of his fair share now," she reports.

However, Liz is the first one to tell you she has not used the best judgment when it comes to handling the man she is still obsessed with. There are some minor indications of progress, she notes.

"Having him live with me and my two children has been a real strain at times. It is hard to be on your best behavior while you are taking care of the kids, the house, and your business and trying to be a lover carrying on a romance. I hesitate to ask Hank to run car pools or help with dinner, but I do ask him to go to the cleaners for me. He has always come first. I am trying to change that."

Liz is hanging on:

1. She is crazy for Hank.

2. She is a firm believer that there are too few decent men out there. She claims to have had enough blind dates to verify that.

3. She feels there is a little more security in the relationship with Hank living in the house rather than a dating situation. After all, during heated arguments, he is the one that threatens he would leave if only he had his own apartment.

4. She still holds on to the belief that they are closer to marriage and that maybe someday they will be a happy family unit.

The key question is whether or not Liz is moving productively toward that goal.

She may have answered her own question when she told me, "I was out to dinner with Hank, my children, and other family members a few nights ago. I noticed and admired at another table a mother, father, and kids that looked so happy. I had to laugh to myself thinking how that image compared with my own and the tension I felt at our table because of Hank."

A Way of Settling for Less

Janice, the woman at the beginning of the chapter who hoped she would remarry at an age younger than eighty, has been involved with Bradley for more than a decade. They dated one another exclusively for ten years after earlier marriages failed and they had ventured out into the single world for a few years. They purchased a home together and moved in three years ago, planning to wed soon after. On the way to the altar, Janice called off the ceremony.

There were too many trouble spots to be able to proceed smoothly. For one, they had a disagreement over serving pork at the wedding. That may sound inconsequential, but it was incompatible with Janice's religious heritage. Bradley, in turn, felt she had no right to impose her values on him and their guests.

"I didn't go ahead with the marriage because I thought I would be stuck in a life of strife," Janice explains.

In a nutshell that is how Janice and Bradley's stalemate began almost three years ago.

Adversaries or Lovers

The differences between Bradley and her were ones Janice had been aware of for years. In fact, they were the same ones that prevented her from marrying or moving in with Bradley sooner. The intensity of their opposition makes them adversaries as well as lovers.

"It is a relationship that definitely has love and mutual respect in it. He is an extremely principled person and truly is my best friend when he isn't my enemy," concedes Janice in the secondmost teary-eyed interview I conducted. "It is a difficult match. The only thing we have in common is our attraction to each other."

Their points of departure are all too apparent. "Bradley represents a different world than the world my children and I are from, and it creates a lot of strife and self-doubt for me," Janice explains. "Before the children left for college, we both knew it would be a very uncomfortable position for all of us to try to live under one roof. I realize now that when I defended my children and their lifestyle, I was and still am really defending myself.

"Bradley and I are not from the same socioeconomic and ethnic backgrounds and do not share all of the same values. I come from a conservative, affluent suburb and a protected childhood. During my first marriage, I was well established in the community and enjoyed country club living. Bradley is the quintessential liberal intellectual who has little use for social camaraderie, materialism, or community affiliations of any kind. Because of my own ambivalence, I have been straddling both worlds ever since I have known him.

"We each get just enough out of living together to stay. However, living with Bradley gives me as much pain as it does pleasure," Janice admits sadly. "He has such a strong set of ethics that it is intimidating. He makes a career out of judging people and situations.

At the same time, he is more fascinating and interesting than anyone else I can imagine. I think to please him I have to compromise more."

Janice acknowledges that her own ambivalence is the most problematic to her. "It is painful that I can't totally commit to this relationship or to leaving it. I think if we were to totally commit, we would be married."

Her ambivalence is admittedly forged by her fear of being alone and the pain she would face in separating. But, more important, it is based upon her inability to reconcile the kind of husband Bradley would make with her own expectations of a lifelong mate.

"Living together allows me to not face some of the problems in our relationship," Janice admits. "If we were married, I would expect Bradley to participate more in the relationship and be more of a couple. I am afraid he wouldn't be able to deliver. That would be an intolerable situation for me. I would expect him to be more accepting of my friends, which he can't seem to do. I am disappointed that he doesn't like people who have loved me and shown me so much friendship and support. I would want Bradley to go places with me instead of always having to make excuses for him and showing up alone.

"We had a discussion about a week ago about being a couple and presenting yourself that way to the world. He had no idea what I meant and said it was the most superficial thing he had ever heard of. Attitudes like that make me disappointed in him. He senses that, and we both end up angry. There are days that I am glad I'm here, and it seems like everything will be fine. I just can't put ten of those days together in a row.

"I know it sounds like an impossible situation, but I hate to admit that," Janice comments. "My friends say that we should get married so that I can get divorced and get this over with already. They say if I had done this when we moved in, I would be starting over already."

Instead, the limbo continues day after day.

◆　◆　◆

Lulled into Complacency by the Comforts of Live-In Love

Patsy and Jack aren't going anywhere. Jack controls the game. He is comfortable just the way things are.

The Twentysomething Chase

This couple began their six-year live-in relationship in their early twenties after a brief but intense long-distance romance shortly after college graduation. They provide each other with all the creature comforts—monogamous sex, good home cooking, nurturing, care-taking, companionship, and economic security. Characteristic of the twentysomething stalemate is Patsy's wish to marry and Jack's wish to stay single.

"Basically, I guess it's me that is holding up getting married," Jack says with little discomfort. "Patsy would have gotten married three years ago if it were up to her. I know that getting married would make her ecstatically happy. She set deadlines in her mind to be married that have come and gone. She teases me that we'll probably get married when we're ninety. There is a little tension. But it is one of those things I'm not going to do until I'm ready. She always asks me what scares me about marriage."

What is holding Jack back? "I'm hesitating for a few reasons," he says.

1. "I am not 100% sure. I guess you never are. I dated another girl for four years before I met Patsy. She abruptly changed her mind and broke things off. That is something that sticks in my mind. I thought she was really in love with me."
2. "I'm not so sure that right now I want to deal with the fact that we are different religions, and we would have to if we were getting married."
3. "I hesitate over the finality of marriage."
4. "I just can't picture myself married."
5. "I'm not sure if I am in love with Patsy. I'm not sure what that means."

Why does Patsy endure the limbo? We'll have to take Jack's

word for that. He preferred I not interview her. "I'm not sure what she would say, and the possibility that she isn't getting enough satisfaction out of this relationship makes me uncomfortable," says Jack without trepidation. He assumes she sticks around because she cares and has invested time and energy in the relationship. It has also probably helped that while she has been unemployed for the last eighteen months, Jack has made sure she is comfy and cozy. Under these circumstances, it appears unlikely that Jack will have to make a move.

In fact, it arouses Jack's ire just to be asked how he would respond to an ultimatum from Patsy. "I would take it as a character flaw or a weakness in her if she said, 'Marry me or I am leaving.' Who knows what else would be buried in her mind?"

Aside from the comforts she provides, Jack makes it sound as if Patsy does not have much bargaining power with which to plan her strategy in this game of cat and mouse. She is merely keeping herself in play, waiting as comfortably as possible to see what the cat's next move will be.

Hiding behind Issues and Answers When Looking for Love

If you have to ask what it means to be in love, chances are you're not. That seems to be a major part of Jack's indecision to move ahead and break the stalemate that he and Patsy are experiencing.

If you have to work at falling in love with your live-in companion, chances are you won't. And capturing the elusive, unexplainable passionate love with Donna is precisely what Billy has tried to do over their four years together.

Can Billy find love in their therapist's office? Or is that the place he hopes to develop the courage to admit the truth?

Examining the Limbo

Billy and Donna had known each other through family friends for several years. When twenty-seven-year-old Donna moved to town, Billy casually extended his hospitality for her to crash at his place. Like many other men, he did not realize how easily a temporary arrangement becomes semi-permanent. It was innocent enough, Billy thought, despite Donna's apparent crush on him. He was, after all, involved in a hot and heavy love affair that had ended his thirteen-year marriage. Donna, however, had more than a mild infatuation. She wanted to have a relationship with this very good-looking charmer several years her senior.

"We kind of connected. In some ways, we are like two peas in a pod. I love sharing things with her. We have the same aesthetic outlook and appreciation of things," Billy says, describing the onset of their live-in relationship.

"Our relationship never was based on sex but on friendship," says Donna, adding to the picture.

But something is missing.

Donna and Billy agree that a number of factors prevent their live-in relationship from moving forward toward the commitments of matrimony and children Donna wants. It isn't something either one of them ignores; they have been trying to resolve significant problems since Donna's discovery that Billy was on the verge of an affair two years ago.

"I was really hurt and upset. I was floored," says Donna, her voice quivering slightly. "I had complete trust in him. Finding out about the other woman made me look back and wonder if he had really been where he said he was in the past. I told him we needed a counselor and went right to the phone book and picked someone out. The therapist we went to said that Billy *wanted* me to find out about this other woman. He was so lax in covering his tracks."

Billy was purposely trying to bring about some change in the relationship. It appears that the same old gridlock is, however, still in place despite the progress in personal insights and personal growth.

"If I could do it over again," says Donna, "I would go through the steps of dating and allow more time for Billy and me to get to know each other. I would have taken my time before moving in. Now we are going backwards and have to grapple with all those things that should have been covered in the first place. We never really got past the introductory stage of talking. We never started communicating and sharing our feelings during the first two years.

We just drifted along."

She admits she gave Billy all of the power and control early in the relationship. "I never felt like it was an equal partnership," she says. "I didn't assert myself. I didn't tell him that having children was important to me, nor that what bothered me the most was when someone would ask us when we were going to get married because I was waiting for Billy to make all of the decisions. I have made it clear that I want children in my life. Now I am waiting for Billy to decide if that's what he wants, too."

But Billy seems to lack that spark, that essential feeling of being in love. "I used to feel that there was something terribly wrong with me because Billy didn't want to marry me," Donna recalls. But she believes he can capture that loving feeling if he will just open himself up emotionally.

"I am probably the one who feels more in love with Billy, but I'm wondering if it is more a need of mine," she says.

Billy is less analytical and more noticeably emotional. His turmoil and the gravity of the decision he must make obviously weigh heavily upon him, as does his lack of sexual passion.

"I have been up front with Donna from the beginning," he avows. "I would do anything in the world for her. It is a really difficult thing to admit that I love her but I am not *in love* with her. For me that is not enough. People ask me, 'What are you doing in the relationship if you aren't in love with her?' I am trying to face that.

"I had an affair before we got together. It was very intense, very powerful and passionate. I was in love the moment I saw this woman. There wasn't that immediate attraction to Donna. Once you have experienced that, you want it again. I don't want to hurt Donna, but I won't marry her without it being there. It is not fair to myself, and she knows it's not fair to her."

Billy describes his lady in respectful, ever-loving terms, but the feeling he wants to recapture keeps eluding him. "Donna has a sort of innocence about her. She is angelic. I love that part of her, but it doesn't excite me sexually. It isn't my ideal of a sexual woman.

"Just getting into the mood to have sex is slow. I could have sex once or twice a day, but we have sex once or twice a week, and it is only moderately satisfying—never a 10. If Donna were a better sex partner, I think our relationship would be better. But I also believe there is a chemistry between two people that needs to be there. It seems odd that I get into bed with Donna, kiss her goodnight, and that's it. To me that is frustrating, because I want that passion to be there for us.

"I don't know if this is a relationship that I want for a lifetime. But I think that the main thing is that we are working on it. I want the relationship to be the best that it can possibly be. That's what it is all about. If I were a betting man, I would give this relationship fifty-fifty odds. If all of the ingredients for the kind of relationship I want were there, I would probably want to have kids."

And so Billy continues the stalemate.

Billy and Donna both report making personal progress in understanding and expressing their emotions, and both appear to have a very sincere desire to make this relationship work. But it is a frustrating and time consuming process for both.

"I don't want to spend the rest of my life thinking about this," acknowledges Billy.

As for Donna, she says, "I went to our therapist the other day and told her time was up. I asked her, 'When do we get our diploma?' It is hard, though, to put a time limit on it. I am changing and taking more responsibility for my life. But to be honest, even if Billy says he doesn't want children, I don't know if I will be able to walk away from him."

And will therapy make it possible for Billy to decide whether the issue of children is the core issue for him? Will therapy help him resolve his own conflict and confusion? Will therapy help him to fall in love with Donna, reclaiming that fiery passion he remembers and desires? Only Billy can answer these questions and end the stalemate that painfully plagues him and Donna, making their love a bittersweet affair.

COUPLES WHO BREAK THE STALEMATE

Here is an introduction to a few very different couples. For one, breaking a six-year stalemate was an exciting exercise in change. For another, it meant shedding youthful loves and moving on. For the third, it meant an end to a nine-year bumpy road on the way to maturity and self-discovery.

Being Liberated from Live-in Love

Pauline and Scott were twenty-four and twenty-six, respectively, when they moved in together as the kind of artistic bohemians that used to be the stereotypical live-in lovers before cohabitation rose to such widespread popularity in the past few decades. They had known each other through graduate school and were committed lovers with a meeting of the minds and hearts.

"We had difficulty just planning for our individual futures," explains Scott. "Marriage was much too abstract a concept then and didn't seem necessary. It wasn't a problem for either of us. Pauline just wanted to know if it was out of the question in the future." Scott goes on to say that they couldn't even have imagined a wedding ceremony that would fit their unconventional tastes.

Pauline had her own concern. She was vacillating between her feminist agenda and her more romantic tendencies, which she feared could have drawn her into a conventional lifestyle to the detriment of her art and her development. Living with Scott enabled her to see that she did not have to compromise her art for the type of marriage relationship they would have.

The passage of time, say Pauline and Scott, afforded them the opportunity to get to know the best and worst about each other and to adjust to their differences. With slow but steady progress in their careers, Scott felt more in control of the future and ready for a change in the relationship. Pauline had no problem agreeing.

"Living together seemed too familiar and predictable to me to go on that way," expresses Scott. "It was drab. All the couples we knew were the eternal boyfriend-girlfriend pair, and we were tired of it. Marriage actually seemed sort of liberating to me. We had spent so much time trying to define ourselves and our relationship. Living together is complicated and puts a strain on you; marriage is simple. Getting married was like saying, 'Okay, now we are a couple.' Why carry on the pretense of being a couple by living together? Marriage concluded the discussion and enabled us to move on."

Pauline's assessment of their new marriage: "The future is full of time to be together. That is one of the things I most look forward to."

Growing Up Sometimes Means Growing Out of a Relationship

Adam and Louise helped one another during a difficult time in their lives, but Adam grew up and out of the live-in relationship.

"We were basically two kids when we moved in together," asserts Adam. "We were in our early twenties. We were two kids who had come from privileged homes void of the emotional support we needed for our development. Louise was anorexic and had dyslexia. She needed comfort and love. So did I.

"There were a lot of things coming down on me at the time. My parents were going through a divorce, and I decided not to attend Harvard Business School, although it was something that was expected of me. Louise and I created a family environment for each other based upon acceptance. We were two kids kind of growing up confused and trying to make sense out of it all. Louise gave me a lot of strength, courage, and support. She couldn't get her own life together, though.

"When I got a job offer in the Midwest some years later, she went with me. She couldn't hang in the public arena, and I was heavy into business by this time. She was a very needy person, and I will admit to some degree I fostered that. I knew I had to end it and tried to be fair, but when I told her she ran down the hall screaming at me that I had wrecked her life. I moved out of my own condominium to give her time to get adjusted. I was paying $1,300 a month for her to live there. She was still there almost two years later. I couldn't afford to keep her place and mine. I became frustrated and impatient to end this chapter of my life. I moved back into my condo and insisted she move out on her own. She did, six months later."

Self-Discovery and an Affirmation of Love

It took nine years of a live-in relationship for Tobey and Hugh to resolve their differences. The finale was a wedding ceremony that had been debated for years.

Tobey was only twenty when she moved in with Hugh, eight years her senior. Moving in was an ironclad case of the "Knight in Shining Armor" Syndrome and followed the classic pattern: Tobey needed a protector during her college years. Hugh rescued her and became controlling and possessive. The years together passed swiftly but not without conflict. Tobey had a few indiscretions, which she confessed to Hugh, and a few doubts about their relationship, which she kept to herself.

"It concerned me that I had not dated very much. I wasn't sure if he fit this ideal of the ultimate man I was looking for," she admits with tears filling her eyes and her hands moving nervously. "I wanted him to be able to talk about the philosophy I was reading or be interested in the plays I was seeing. I thought maybe I had picked the wrong person. Education is very important to me. I graduated magna cum laude, and Hugh had not been to college. I couldn't say that I loved him more than anything else in the world. I knew he tried to make me feel guilty for my feelings by saying he would never love anyone but me."

Despite her confusion, Hugh proposed after year six. Tobey bought a wedding dress and started to plan the nuptials for the beginning of year eight. When she and I sat down to talk early in that year, she had just postponed her walk down the aisle.

"He is my best friend, and I can't imagine life without him," she said. "I feel so guilty. I don't know if I am with him because he gives security and unconditional love or because of who he is. But I am not sure what it is that I want. If I were stronger, more sure of myself, I would know I am making my own choice to be with him. I need to spend time thinking about who I am."

That is exactly what Tobey did for six months, with the help of a counselor. Once she discovered, without Hugh's influence, what it was she thought would make her happy, she told him, "I *want* to marry you."

When I spoke with her weeks after her wedding, she was a bubbly, gushing bride.

SHAKING UP THE STATE
OF PERPETUAL LIMBO

It is difficult to face the reality of a live-in love relationship that looks like it is going nowhere. Indeed, as we have seen, a number of men and women prefer to invent excuses and rationalizations that perpetuate the game of cat and mouse. Fearful of consequences and unsure of their own goals, they skirt the cumbersome issues that might result in separation.

Abundant evidence of the stalemate of live-in love and the characteristics that identify it have been amply provided in this chapter. For those who acknowledge their game of cat and mouse and now wish to face the stalemate, here are a few suggestions on how to proceed, from other live-in lovers who were willing to take the chance:

1. Make a list of the issues that stand in the way of moving your live-in relationship beyond the stalemate. Compare that to your partner's list. Try to develop a consensus and work together on the real issues that stand in the way of your happiness and satisfaction.

2. Take a reality check. Is what you are saying what you are feeling? Make sure they are in sync. Suggest your partner do the same.

3. Make a list of "What ifs." Consider what you would like to say and do to get past the state of limbo you are now experiencing. Carefully measure the consequences. Take a long, hard look at your options, and act.

These are worthwhile suggestions to carry over into the discussion of the old divorce story excuse, to be examined in the next chapter. All too often, those who buy into this excuse find themselves caught in the familiar holding pattern indicative of the stalemate of live-in love.

CHAPTER 5

The Old Divorce Story Excuse

"I'm never getting married again. I'll never put myself in a position to go through another divorce," vow a multitude of men and a much smaller number of women during their post-divorce recovery period. The fact is that plenty do take that chance.

For our investigation the pertinent question with regard to this predominately male-oriented statement is: When a woman moves in with a divorced man because matrimony seems out of the question—at least for the moment—how can she tell if she is getting the old divorce story excuse or the truth?

As men also sometimes hear this excuse, the advice offered in this chapter may also be insightful for them. However, because this more often happens to women, I use the feminine pronoun.

FATAL AND NEAR-FATAL ERRORS WOMEN MAKE

Women who succumb to the divorce story excuse without thoroughly assessing the situation make fatal or near-fatal errors in judgment. Typically this type of person:

• disregards blatant messages from her live-in partner that marriage is not a likely option. She lives in the fairy-tale world of happy endings and is convinced that he will change his mind.

• fails to recognize that her live-in will not commit to a permanent relationship because of his ambivalent feelings toward her. It's
not only his bitterness from a failed marriage or a miserable divorce.

• buys the divorce story excuse too readily, causing herself unnecessary misery and prolonged unhappiness.

ASSESSING THE POTENTIAL TO WED

When a person hopes to marry a live-in lover who gives the divorce story excuse, it is prudent for her to assess the *real* potential
for him to wed. Undeniably this is tricky; however, there are questions to be asked and clues to be uncovered that will assist in this
probe. To begin, it is important to determine the following:

1. How the odds for his remarrying stack up.
2. How divorce affects the course of live-in love.
3. What major stumbling blocks and hurdles need to be overcome to advance toward remarriage.
4. Who is giving this excuse.
5. Which individuals are the least likely to wed.
6. Why many good men and a few good women rely on this
excuse to escape getting married.
7. Which men and women buy the old divorce story.
8. What the real message is behind the old divorce story
excuse.
9. How your lover treats you.

Males Who Are Likely to Remarry:
Encouraging Statistics

Divorced men remarry at a high rate when compared to the
entire adult male population.

Younger divorced males have better odds of becoming someone's husband than do older divorced men. Based upon 1987 figures
published by the National Center for Health Statistics, men in their
late thirties are 60 percent more likely to remarry than men in their
fifties. Another crucial measurement is how long this man has been

on the loose. The longer he is single, the less favorable the odds for remarriage. In 1987, 70 percent of the men who remarried reported being single less than five years, and more than half of the men tied the knot in less than two and a half years.

When determining the likelihood of his remarrying, these are handy statistics to have in mind. However, Barbara Lovenheim, author of *Beating the Marriage Odds*, cautions not to give up completely on divorced men in their forties and fifties who have remained single beyond the five-year period. In 1987, more than 10 percent of those men who remarried at this age took nine years to say, "I do."

For the inquiring male. Women want to remarry. Statistics that show they do so less frequently than men are probably more indicative of the problems women have in finding a suitable mate than an unwillingness to wed.

Too Much Time in the Single Lane

Tony gets right to the heart of this matter and helps us to understand the statistics and why the passage of time diminishes a man's interest in remarrying. He was single for ten years before he became a groom for the second time when he was in his early fifties.

"I think I could have gone on being unmarried for a long period of time. I had really gotten settled into my own routine after my divorce. I think when men who have raised their families get divorced and do not remarry quickly, they realize they can take care of themselves and stay single a long time. Life is not all that complex. You go out and buy a washer and a dryer, hire a cleaning lady, play tennis when you want, and have a variety of women to date, travel with, or have an affair with."

What's Packed in Their Bags?

Men and women who have not yet unpacked the baggage from their first divorce not only present a significant risk factor in the face of live-in love, but are more likely to be sincere when they say, "I won't remarry."

It is worthwhile, therefore, to see what male live-in lovers have to say about their post-divorce era and what lies behind their pervasive pessimism and gloom. Many of them express that they felt:

- disappointment
- trauma
- devastation
- failure
- guilt
- bitterness
- rejection.

Social scientists believe men and women go through a period of grief after a divorce. It is not so much a process of grieving for one's estranged partner as for the loss of comforts, pleasures, and rewards previously incurred from the relationship. And it is not uncommon for individuals to emerge from a broken marriage with diminished self-esteem and a sense of betrayal and distrust. Consequently, men making the transition from married to single life often harbor a jaded attitude toward remarrying. These men may:

- be skeptical of an institution that was supposed to offer a lifetime commitment and didn't.
- view marriage as a hazard to be avoided.
- doubt their own potential to build a lasting relationship.

Howard, involved in a live-in relationship with no plans to wed after childless marriages lasting thirteen and eleven years, is a good example of how divorce makes one highly suspect of matrimony.

"Divorce eats your guts out," says Howard, visibly angry still. "I've been burned twice. Maybe I'm just not the kind of guy to have a relationship. I don't know. I know that it has made me bitter and cost me a lot of money. The first divorce was real messy and had a bad effect on me. I was thrown out of my house and barred from entering by a court order. I *paid* for that house, mind you!"

◆   ◆   ◆

Do Men Mean It When They Say It?

There are some pretty good indications that Howard should be taken at his word. Marriage does not work for him or figure into his future. However, many men use the excuse of failed marriages and tumultuous divorces to maintain live-in relationships and hedge the commitment their lovers seek.

Investigating Howard's story will begin to uncover when to believe and when not to believe the divorce story excuse.

Take Howard at His Word: No to Matrimony

Howard offers plentiful evidence that he is not likely to be a candidate for marriage. Is Becca, his live-in, getting the message?

Howard is a hard-driving businessman who approaches his personal and professional life in the same cold, unemotional, and practical way. Self-sufficient, fiercely independent, and highly opinionated, he is not easily swayed from his line of thinking. His interpretation of his love relationships sounds like a string of business deals.

Here is how Howard dismissed his first marriage: "We got married for the wrong reasons. She was into the baby business, and I was into the money business. We had different values and should have made an agreement on the baby issue before we got married."

Here is how he characterized his second marriage: "That was for fun and companionship. Marie was a highly successful businesswoman who posed no worries about babies. Everything was going fine until her business went downhill and so did our marriage."

Howard's single days fell into two distinct periods. "For a while I was a male slut, waking up in beds that I couldn't even remember having sex in or falling asleep," he confesses.

And then there was the year-and-a-half affair with Judy. "I cared about Judy and came the closest to loving her of any woman. She was innocent and sweet in a way that made me want to protect her. *Her talk of marriage killed the relationship.* This was a very intense relationship, and I learned something from it: Not to do it again. It only disappointed me. I would be reluctant to open myself up like that again," Howard reveals in a matter-of-fact tone of voice.

After Judy, Howard (then forty-nine) met Becca and used his typical businesslike manner to strike a live-in deal. Becca was, after all, suitable for this limited partnership: She was forty-seven years old, widowed without children, bright, pretty, sophisticated, and able to mix with his friends and associates. They dated for just less than a year before Howard asked Becca to move in. That was more than a year and a half ago.

Howard cannot say whether this is a love relationship. "I don't use that word well. I'm not sure what that means anymore," he explained. "I think Becca is in love with me, but she doesn't know if I am with her." Nevertheless, Howard left little room for speculating what was on the table if Becca accepted his invitation. His terms were clearly spelled out.

"I told Becca that I was not willing to uproot myself again to satisfy someone else. I like the place I live in. It is mine. If she wanted to join me there, fine," says Howard, numerically rattling off his conditions.

"I expected to retain my same lifestyle, except that I would be monogamous. I live kind of a loose life. I work crazy hours, play golf, travel, and have drinks with friends when I want to. Furthermore, what I do in terms of my investments is my own business. I don't want any help or any input when it comes to my business affairs. This has no bearing on her. I am prepared to protect her financially and pay all of her living expenses. I don't need to know anything about her income or inherited estate. And I won't tolerate anyone trying to get inside of my head and speculate about my feelings," he concludes adamantly.

Howard is clear about what he wants and what he feels he is getting from his living arrangement with Becca. "I do not feel trapped like I did in marriage," he explains. "I am able to fulfill my own commitment to total financial independence. Secondly, it's nice to have someone to come home to who cares about you. There is a level of comfort associated with having someone in the house.

"I am sure that women reading my point of view might think I am the biggest jerk that ever lived. But they are taking all of this out of context; they should see the flip side.

"I think a woman gets a great deal out of a live-in relationship.

She has all the freedom in the world and no responsibility whatsoever," says Howard, defending his position. "If you set up the rules and proceed accordingly, no one gets the raw end of the deal. I may be tough, but not at Becca's expense.

"When she had elective surgery, I was very caring and waited on her hand and foot. I had a maid come in every day until she recovered. And I may tease her and say I am not getting her a Valentine's gift and then show up with a diamond bracelet. I have even made provisions for Becca in my will.

"My attitude about the relationship may be difficult for Becca at times," acknowledges Howard, "but I make her laugh, and she hasn't done that in a long time. She knows I am competitive and business-minded, and she idolizes and respects that part of me. I want Becca to be happy. I care about what she does, and I support her in her work. I respect her as a person. *It's just that I don't care to do anything about the situation, and I think there's a difference,*" he says, meaning he does not have marriage in mind.

Despite Howard's up-front manner, it sounds like Becca is one of those women who still holds out hope for matrimony.

"When she brings up marriage, I tell her to stow it," says Howard. "I am not marriage material at the moment. I don't think Becca will press the issue enough to make me face whether I ever will be. But if she did say, 'Marry me or I'll move out,' I'd probably reply, 'When do you want to move out?'

"I think every woman in my life has been dispensable," he says with candor. "There is nothing that they provide for me that I can't afford for myself. I can't say this is a forever thing, only that it is long-term. I'm not looking for security. Security isn't even a concern of mine. I don't ask Becca if she feels secure. You don't ask those kinds of questions if you don't want to hear the real answers."

Howard's attitude may be cut and dry to the objective eye. Gregory's excuse to Roz leaves room for interpretation.

Gregory's Excuse Leaves Room for Interpretation

Gregory, a family man if ever there was one, found himself faced with a wife who wanted a divorce after twenty years of what he thought was a happy lifelong partnership. "It came as a real shock to me. I fought for my wife, and up until the divorce I thought she would come to her senses and change her mind. I got burned—really burned—and it was excruciatingly painful," he says, still wondering how his world fell apart.

Shattered by losing the woman he loved, the family he enjoyed, and the orderly life he thrived in, Gregory raised his defenses to ward off the possibility of another deep hurt. "I'm through with marriage," he announces.

Devastated, disillusioned, and disappointed, Gregory was thrust into a single world he was not fully equipped to handle. He started dating immediately, looking for reassurance and approval from women. And he found himself well accepted by a woman who was heading him uncontrollably toward marriage—until forty-year-old Roz came along.

"I'm involved with another woman," he pleaded to his would-be bride, getting himself gracefully out of the relationship. Roz, however, was well versed in live-in love from two previous relationships. Neither had led to marriage. Roz quickly maneuvered herself into his home six months after they started dating.

"Before I knew it, she had moved in. I probably let it happen. I was bound and determined to learn to be independent and live on my own, but I was very lonely and did not find the freedom I had good for me. I realized I needed structure and security in my life," he says, adding that he missed this lifestyle he associated with marriage. "Without it, I was staying out all night and drinking. I wanted a companion and a one-on-one relationship. I thought that I could live comfortably with Roz. It seemed like a convenient arrangement."

On a day-to-day basis, Gregory points out that living together has some of the features of married life: sharing a house, a bed, a bathroom, a kitchen table, and a routine. However, in Gregory's mind, Roz is far from qualifying as his wife.

"I do not see Roz as a member of my family. I want that kind of separation, even though she is trying hard to fit in with my children and my family. She is more like a good friend, but not my best friend. She fills the gap in my life right now, but at times I feel she is infringing on my freedom. I don't like her to plan my activities or call me at the office to see when I will be home. I want to take each day at a time with her. I am not into any long-range planning.

"I have been up front with Roz about marriage. I told her from the beginning, 'Don't come on to me about marriage.' She doesn't totally believe me and feels once I get over the pain of my divorce, I'll change my mind," says Gregory.

"Roz thinks that the reason I haven't told her I love her is that it is difficult for me to say it. But I *don't* love her. There isn't that spark between us. I want to be in a position, free with no strings, to pursue that feeling if it happens with another woman. I believe that there is a right person out there for me, and someday I could find her. There is a chance that I could commit to her for the rest of my life. I guess that is what I am looking for.

"Of course, this is something I don't discuss with Roz," Gregory reveals.

Questions Becca and Roz Should Be Asking

Roz and Becca may both be dangerously close to making fatal errors in judgment. Each remains hopeful that, despite their protests, Gregory and Howard's determination to remain single will wane, increasing their chances to wed.

What these and other women should be doing is evaluating the validity of the divorce story excuse and uncovering the reason behind it. To do this women should ask themselves the following questions. *(Approach the exercise honestly to reveal the truth.)*

1. Did his divorce pose financial and emotional difficulties for him?

The more bitter his separation from his wife and the more emotional his divorce, the more difficulty *you* may have getting a good read on his excuse.

Affirmative answers to questions 2 through 9 give you a good idea where this man might eventually stand on the subject of marriage and where he stands on you. Be prepared that the revelations may be painful.

2. Did he enjoy married life?

3. Is he the marrying kind?

4. Does he have the capacity to love and share his life?

5. Is there evidence that he loves you?

6. Does he verbalize or clearly demonstrate that he sees this as a permanent relationship?

7. Are you very important to him?

8. Does he treat you like part of the family?

9. Does he ever mention marrying you?

The last question is the toughest. Roz didn't see the answer. Would you?

10. Is it me he doesn't want to commit to, or is it marriage?

These ten questions could help the next group of women focus more clearly on their dilemmas as well.

Old Excuses, New Promises

The time comes when sympathy and understanding are no longer as beneficial as action. As the recipient of the divorce story excuse, it might be time to say, *"Hey, mister, forget your other relationship and forget the excuse already. We're talking about me and you here!"*

Roxanne and Molly's stories prove that might be the case, even though they were a little off of their timing. These two made near-fatal errors in judgment by accepting the old excuse too easily and for too long.

Not Knowing When to Make Her Move

Roxanne's Alex is a lot like Howard: independent, self-sufficient, and a businessman all the way. He lost half of his sizable personal wealth in his divorce settlement and wanted to make sure that never happened again. Alex also vowed not to marry until he made the last installment on his ten-year payoff plan to his ex-wife. Despite the similarities in personality and the use of the notorious excuse, Alex's history with Roxanne is a whole different game than Howard and Becca's.

Since his divorce five years earlier, Alex, at forty-two, was having the time of his life being a swinging single with an abundance of women, substantial financial resources, and unrestricted freedom. He was not looking for love but found it anyway on a blind date with Roxanne, thirteen years his junior, divorced, and the mother of two young daughters.

They dated for two years, enjoying each other's company with no commitment until Alex decided to change businesses. An out-of-state move prompted both of them to evaluate the importance of their relationship and to determine if they were willing to be separated by several hundred miles.

"Neither one of us wanted to get married then," Alex explains, "but Roxanne was astute enough to know that she better not let me leave the city without her. She hesitated to uproot her children and move without some type of commitment.

"I said, 'Okay, let's get engaged.' It seemed more respectable to give her a reason to come with me. In reality, I got engaged to make life easier. It was an okay thing to do without taking the relationship too seriously.

"We were getting along pretty well for a year and a half after the move. She lived around the corner. But then I had a heavy flirtation with another woman. 'After all,' I said, justifying my behavior to myself, 'I am still single, and I'm not even living with someone.' Roxanne was really hurt and thought I was having an affair. She recognized that she was more vulnerable than she realized. The episode made me see that here was a really good woman in my life who meant a lot to me. In my mind I resolved that I was going to marry her."

But Alex was not so resolved as to set a date.

"Her perception of an affair triggered my suggestion that we live together and, at some point later, talk about marriage. The odds by this time were pretty good that I would *eventually* marry Roxanne. I told her up front that I was going to be careful about this and would require her to sign a premarital agreement. When we combined households, I was turning fifty and Roxanne planned a huge party for my birthday. She wasn't completely sold on moving in without being married and wanted us to have a wedding ceremony the weekend of the party.

"I refused and could tell she was quite upset. I was trying to mentally prepare myself for remarrying, and I wasn't going to let anyone talk me into it." Alex says, admitting he was guilty of relying on the divorce story excuse. "I hadn't hit the ten-year mark yet, and I wasn't prepared to be monogamous for the rest of my life at that time.

"Roxanne accepted my excuses too easily," Alex admits in retrospect. "She should have said something like, 'I would love to live with you. We have a wonderful relationship. I think it would be great for us. But if we are going to do it, particularly since my children live with me, we have to be married. If you are not ready to get married, then we can still be what we are in our life, but we can't live together.' I think that point would really have pulled my chain at that time. I think I would have married her then."

The relationship started a downhill trend after he said, "No."

Roxanne, not so quick to forgive and forget by this time, had a terrible auto accident that resulted in a year's convalescence. Unlike so many life-and-death situations that produce greater love and appreciation for a couple, the stress affected Roxanne and Alex's relationship adversely. After her recuperation, the pair lived open and separate while under the same roof. Roxanne did not stick around for long. She was through with Alex, through with living together, through with waiting, through with his infidelities. She was feeling and looking great inside and out.

Once she was gone, Alex wanted her back. He was jealous for the first time in his life, he admits. When she moved in again within the year, it was as his wife. They have been happily married for over three years now and continue to work on their relationship with the help of a family therapist.

Why Molly Waited to Walk Out

"I was too patient with him," Molly says eight years after she and Tony became involved. "I don't think he would have been as patient if the table had been turned. He promised we would get married, but for almost the last four years he's said he hasn't been ready.

I accepted that until I had had enough."

This is the new Molly speaking. The old one would never have recognized such an error in judgment.

Married and divorced, Molly was in her early twenties when she became romantically attached to Tony. He was twelve years older, her boss, a good friend, and stuck in a very unhappy marriage. Six months after he and Molly started dating, Tony separated from his wife. It doesn't come across clearly who insisted on the split, only that neither the Mr. nor the Mrs. was faithful to the other.

According to Molly, "Tony was very hurt by the divorce. It ruined him financially, and it undermined his relationship with his son, leaving them both scarred emotionally. Tony said that marriage changed his relationship with his wife and that she became bitchy and demeaning. He's afraid that what happened to him before could happen again."

Molly was full of sympathy and understanding for the first four years of their romance. Without hesitation she traipsed off to Tony's home almost every night to share his bed without contemplating the future of their relationship.

"I found somebody who was right for me," she says. "By the time I moved into Tony's condo, we were seriously committed to each other, but we had not discussed marriage. It wasn't until a year later when we decided to buy a house together, which required my financial contribution, that I approached the subject. That's when I asked him, 'Why should I give you money for a house that isn't even mine when there is no commitment here?' He responded by giving me a diamond ring."

He did not respond with a wedding date.

At our first meeting, Molly wanted to convey the message that she was completely happy. "Tony always tells me he loves me. We have a great relationship and are absolutely each other's best friend," she said eagerly. "We come home from work and sit together in one chair in this big house. He is an honest person, and I trust him."

But shortly after this tale began, tears formed in this very pretty young woman's eyes. "Now you are making me upset," she remarked when asked about a wedding date.

"Well, actually, I should tell you. I gave the ring back a few weeks ago," she confesses. "I am tired of people telling me how pretty the ring is and asking me when we are getting married. I am tired of feeling like the mistress. Business acquaintances we see year after year don't even know my name. I went to visit my parents and my brother and realized everyone had their own family. I want Tony and I to be a family. He knows I came into this whole thing thinking we would be married. It makes me feel like there is something wrong with me.

"After seven years, it just hit me that I was nowhere. I told Tony that I knew he was playing games with me and that I wanted a wedding date by my birthday. I'll be thirty in a few months. I won't wear the ring until then."

Checking in with Molly shortly after her birthday, I noticed the ring was back on her finger. Tony may have given her flowers and an extra dose of sweetness but again set no date. She excused his behavior and told me, "I know he won't make any false promises. He doesn't know when he will be ready to get married. I can't imagine having this kind of relationship with anyone else."

More than nine months later when we sat down to talk for the final time, Molly acknowledged that Tony had been dragging his feet on the marriage issue. With a new sense of confidence and authority she described what had transpired a few months earlier. It changed the course of her relationship; she was now in the midst of making plans for a wedding.

"It was midsummer," Molly explains, "and I was disgusted and depressed. The anger was building and building inside of me. I was sick of Tony's attitude. I got to a point where I was totally frustrated with my job and with him. I couldn't go on the way it was. One day I exploded at work, quit my job, and started packing my bags. Tony came home and found me loading the car.

"I told him I was leaving. It was the first time I said it and meant it. He knew it and told me, 'Pick a date. I can't live without you. I'll never let you go. You never said, "Marry me or I'm leaving."'

"I should have done it sooner," Molly says. "I can see now that he did not *have* to make a commitment to be before. I never gave him an ultimatum that I truly meant.

"I never knew for sure until now whether we would be married or not," she concludes without a trace of tears. "Mine is a happy ending."

TAKING THE NEXT STEP

While we wish Molly all the best of luck, there is much evidence in the next chapter that suggests a walk down the aisle after a live-in relationship is still no guarantee of a happy ending.

CHAPTER 6

A Gloomy Marriage Forecast

"Are you sure? It's hard to believe." That is invariably the response from men and women when they hear the facts about live-in love, marriage, and divorce.

But it is not fiction that:

- statistics reveal a greater than 50 percent higher incidence of divorce among couples who cohabited than those who did not prior to marriage.
- living together does not act as a test of compatibility for marriage.
- many couples who lived together prior to marriage report rocky marital relationships.

What's behind the number of divorces? There is not just one simple answer to this question.

FAILURE TO BELIEVE IN
THE PERMANENCE OF MARRIAGE

Researchers pinpoint the cause of divorce as specific attitudes they believe are held by people who choose cohabitation over more traditional living arrangements. For instance, Professors William G.

Axinn of the University of Chicago and Arland Thornton of the University of Michigan conclude:

1. Couples who cohabit exhibit less of a commitment to marriage than couples who do not live together before marriage.

2. Live-in relationships add validity to the belief that love relationships are temporary, lowering expectations for achieving a life-long partnership and substantially increasing acceptance of divorce by those who cohabit.

3. Younger men and women who express a strong commitment to marriage are less likely to live together before exchanging vows.

While it is worthwhile to consider this genre of explanations, there is ample evidence from the individuals I interviewed that these are only partial answers. Approximately 75 percent of these middle- to upper-middle-class men and women endorsed the institution of marriage, even if they had participated in a less committed live-in relationship. Consequently, we must search for more answers.

LIVING TOGETHER MAY BE A POOR SPRINGBOARD FOR MARRIAGE

Couples who cohabit, marry, and then divorce frequently fall into matrimony, misread their live-in partners, and fail to resolve significant issues before becoming husband and wife. Living together is not a true test of their compatibility.

Falling into Marriage

The momentum that builds from living together may sweep incompatible couples to the altar prematurely.

Case 1: Moving Too Quickly Can Spell Disaster

"We dated for a year and a half and had lived together for three months when we became engaged. I don't think we would have gotten engaged so quickly, but Shelley's parents did not know we were living together," says Norman, then a recent college graduate. "I got tired of the ridiculous games we had to play answering the phone to hide our arrangement. It was easier to make an official commitment to each other. In reality, I thought that what we had committed to was sharing the same address, but Shelley and her parents insisted on setting a wedding date. I was trapped after that.

"Maybe I didn't notice the things that were wrong when we lived together because I was out of town so much with my new job. I thought if we did marry we would be able to make a home together and build a future. Shelley, however, was still in college when we married and turned out to be totally immature. She assumed no responsibility in caring for our apartment and did not like it that I worked so hard. I think she became bored with our relationship. In less than a year, I found out she was having an affair."

Even if Norman had wanted to delay or cancel the wedding, he may not have been able to do so. Caroline couldn't.

Case 2: Lacking the Courage to Turn Back

Caroline, embroiled in a rebellious live-in affair at twenty years old, is one of those young women who fell into marriage. Sitting at the Thanksgiving table discussing her sister's wedding, she suddenly found herself making plans for a double wedding. "It wouldn't have been that easy to jump in if we weren't living together," she admits today. "We thought we loved each other but never seriously gave marriage the kind of consideration we should have. My ex-husband never got down on his knees and said, 'Marry me. I love you more than life.'

"Once the wedding invitations were out, I decided he was crazy and realized he had a serious drinking problem. I actually ran away. I was afraid of him," says this pretty, soft-spoken young woman. "I didn't want to go through with the marriage, but I had my wedding gown and the invitations were already out. My mother said I would have to call everyone we invited and personally tell them why there would be only one daughter getting married. I wouldn't do it. I thought, 'I'll just get divorced.'"

That is exactly what Caroline did one year later.

Misreading Your Live-In, Tying The Knot

When you fail to develop an accurate picture of your live-in partner, he or she will undoubtedly be a surprise package—for better or for worse—upon becoming your spouse.

Despite opinions to the contrary, it is *easy* to misread your live-in partner, particularly when:

* you are a poor judge of character
* you close your eyes to the real picture
* you do not ask the right questions
* he/she is on his/her best behavior
* he/she deliberately deceives you.

Case 1: What You See is Not What You're Getting

A year and a half after his wife of twenty-one years died, Sanford fell in love. This is the Barbie he thought he was moving in with nine months later: She was nearly ten years younger, beautiful, sexy, sweet, loving, honest, a college grad with honors, the picture of domesticity, a gourmet cook, full of charm, and kind and nurturing to his children.

Smitten by this image, he says, "Although we weren't engaged when Barbie moved in, I already had it in my mind that we would be married." Barbie gave him no reason to change his mind before he married a year later.

During their live-in period, she ended his daily dilemma of what to feed his son, who still lived at home. She provided warm companionship and great sex. She made him proud with her holiday meals, which she graciously served to his extended family. She took an interest in his son, driving him around, shopping with him, and seeing to his needs. She worked on having a reasonable relationship with his daughter, who lived out of town and resisted Barbie's attention. And Barbie tried and succeeded at being on her very best behavior.

Sanford, who suggested the name Barbie for his ex-wife's alias in this story, said, "She was, in fact, as plastic as the Barbie doll in the toy store. Let me tell you, it is easy for someone to be on their good behavior for six months, a year, or even two years. *It is a bunch of baloney that someone can't put on a great act living together if they think they can get something out of the living arrangement."*

He acknowledges that after a good marriage, he was conditioned to believing and trusting women. "I never knew a woman who lied continually," he says, explaining his naiveté at the time. "And I wanted to believe everything Barbie told me. I didn't like being single, and I wanted to get married. I wasn't looking for things that were wrong with the relationship when she moved in."

It came as quite a shock when the real Barbie stepped forward.

For starters, the job she said she was offered in Chicago and would take unless they married quickly was pure fantasy. The big deal she was working on for his public relations firm was a hoax. She held no college degree, let alone one with honors. The thousands of dollars she took to the bank never showed up on Sanford's statements of deposit. And she was not a sweet, blonde Barbie stepmother.

"As soon as we were married, she stopped paying attention to my son and declared open warfare on my daughter. She said I had never told her that we couldn't adopt a child, even though we had agreed on never *having* children. She absolutely became mean and hysterical, screaming and scratching me at times. She repeatedly threatened that unless we adopted, she would have nothing to do with my kids or my future grandchildren.

"That's when I had to draw the line," explains Sanford.

After two years of marriage and one year of living in his sumptuous home, Barbie—showing her real colors—was not pulling out easily.

"The state where I reside requires either the husband or the wife to be out of the house for thirty days before you can file for divorce," says Sanford. "I was not about to leave my own home. The only way I knew I could get her out was to contrive a story about my daughter moving back home. I knew Barbie would never live under the same roof with her, so I asked my daughter to write a detailed letter to me about coming home and purposely left it lying around."

Obviously Sanford had gotten Barbie's number. The letter did the trick, but the disillusion cost him $100,000. Sanford wished he had bumped into one of Barbie's previous boyfriends before he ever asked her to move in. "You should have called me up for a reference," this man told Sanford, not surprised by what had transpired between Sanford and Barbie.

Case 2: Assuming the Best, Hiding the Worst

Alicia thought she was worldly and wise when it came to men. By the age of thirty she had experienced marriage, divorce, and a long-term affair. She thought she was prepared to handle her latest love relationship with Torrance, a recent widower old enough to be her father.

When he asked her to move in after dating for five months, she said okay, if they became engaged. She accepted his explanation that he had some business to clean up before he could marry and his bargain—marriage, no kids, and no interfering in his business.

"Everything was perfect," recalls Alicia. "We had this wonderful little life. We went places, had fun, enjoyed each other's company. He painted a beautiful picture of his close family relationship and his comfortable, secure lifestyle. I should have noticed that he kept his children at arm's length and that he was always off putting mysterious business deals together.

"We set a wedding date, but I wasn't allowed to tell anyone that we had married until a month after the fact. I had no idea why. It upset me that I couldn't tell my parents."

Once the cat was out of the bag, Alicia realized why he wanted to keep the news a secret. She assumed his children would give a big party in honor of their father's marriage. Their reactions hardly met her expectations. "His children absolutely would not accept me. They cursed and screamed at me and called me a piece of garbage. And then they refused to ever talk to me or acknowledge my presence. I thought we would be a happy family and that I would be given that opportunity to enjoy their babies, since I would never have my own. The worst was that my husband didn't even stand up for me."

Those weren't the only illusions from her live-in days that faded away into reality. "He turned into one of the most negative people I ever met," explains Alicia.

Gone were the fun and games. "I was to cook, clean, keep him happy sexually, work, and be at the country club to socialize with women thirty years older than myself. Not only did I find out quickly enough that he had serious financial problems that might involve illegalities, but he was ill on top of everything."

Alicia would have been better prepared for marriage after live-in love if she had asked some pretty tough questions during those days. *Instead, she assumed the best and saved the questions for her divorce.*

Failing to Resolve Major Issues

Trouble is a certainty when couples dismiss the importance of conflicts that erupt while living together and fail to resolve them before stepping into marriage.

Areas of potential conflict include the baby issue, lifestyle, money, your partner's kids, your kids, and sex. Don't assume five years of maturity will change her mind about having kids, when you are certain you want to be a family man and she says she has no desire to be a mom. Don't assume he won't put up a fuss if you take a full-time job when he tells you he wants a woman who stays at home. Don't assume, like Cyril, that he will turn into a lover when you wed if the passion isn't there living together.

Too many couples make shaky assumptions.

Case 1: There Is No Substitute for Sex

Cyril, at twenty-eight, moved in with Joshua four months after they met. "It was one of those cases that I moved to Tampa because I was in love with him like no one before. I was very attracted to Joshua. He was fun and had a great sense of humor. We built a good friendship that is intact today. I knew he was the kind of man I wanted to marry. Sex was our problem," she says without hesitation.

"There were times before I moved to Tampa that I would visit him and we would not make love. I wasn't sex-driven, but I was crazy about him and dying to sleep with him. I thought it was rather strange that a weekend would go by without sex.

"When I moved in, we didn't make love frequently enough for a new young couple in love—maybe not even once a week. I was afraid if I said something after we became engaged six months later he would change his mind about getting married. All my friends were married, and my parents were pushing me. I thought things would get better after we got married. Our wedding was only months away.

"I was the first one to change the rules once we married, but our sex life didn't change. I am embarrassed to tell you that sometimes we would make love once a month and always at my instigating. I finally asked him why we didn't make love more often. He said he just didn't get aroused. I told him it really bothered me and asked him to go to a clinic for sexual dysfunctions. Joshua had no problem with that. He was more than willing to go. He was a real doll about it.

"We found out that he had an incredibly low sex drive," explains Cyril. She might have found some consolation in knowing that approximately one out of every five adults is not interested in having sex. "We were given exercises that had to do with touching. I had to remind Joshua and urge him to do them with me. I am a touchy, feely person and was so in love with Joshua that I felt terribly rejected and frustrated by our lack of sex. It was humiliating to always be the one to initiate sex. A close friend and confidant told me to have an affair. I couldn't. Instead I went to a psychiatrist to determine if I could spend the rest of my life like that.

"In the meantime," Cyril continues, "I stopped taking the pill because we were making love so infrequently. Of course, I got pregnant. I was so pissed; we hadn't even made love in six weeks. I wanted to have a child, but not now. I knew it would force me to stay married. Joshua wanted the child but agreed to go with me anyway to get an abortion.

"Finally, a year later, when we were to move into the house we had just renovated, I couldn't go with him," Cyril says with resignation. "We had been married three years and I couldn't take it anymore. *Nothing he did could make up for our lack of a sexual relationship.*"

SETTING POOR PRECEDENTS FOR SATISFYING MARITAL RELATIONSHIPS

The divorce statistics from live-in lovers do not include the couples who nearly split or who experience rocky marital relationships. Their problems often stem from the live-in days when they failed to establish:

+ an equitable relationship
+ positive roles
+ prudent guidelines for behavior
+ reality-based expectations
+ a meaningful foundation for a lasting relationship.

These poor precedents send aftershocks into the marital relationship and sabotage the transition to husband and wife.

Need proof? Here are two cases.

Live-In Love, On and Off Again Before and After Marriage

Cynthia's saga began when she was twenty-eight and started dating Ted. She had six years of a career under her belt and her own money, car, and furniture. Ted, twenty-nine years of age, was divorced, affluent, spoiled, the father of two children, and involved with a young college student.

"I was looking for excitement in a relationship and found a bomb ready to go off," Cynthia says.

Moving In Before Ted Finished His Romantic Attachment to a Younger Woman

"There was a chemistry between us. We talked about marriage during the two years we dated, but Ted was not ready to commit even though he disliked living alone. He wasn't even ready to be monogamous, but he wanted to be with somebody. If it wasn't me who moved in, it would have been someone else. It was a costly, stupid mistake," Cynthia admits, getting ready to recount years of turmoil.

90

"I was torn in two directions by my heart and my mind. Who knows what goes through your head when you say, 'I'm going for this one'? I moved in because I hoped the next step would be marriage. It was Ted's idea to live together instead of marrying right away. 'Let's see how it goes,' he told me.

"It didn't go well. There were tremendous emotional highs and lows for me. He kept me guessing and called all of the shots. I was put in a position where I was totally scrutinized by his family and a tight-knit ethnic community. This produced static between us. I was at a distinct disadvantage from the beginning."

This wasn't the only reason for discord with this pair. Ted had not completely broken off his relationship with the young college girl who had caused the final disintegration of his marriage a year before. The scandalous affair between a then high-school student and a member of a prominent family was a huge embarrassment and not something to flaunt in public.

"She definitely played a part in our problems," Cynthia states. "If she had just left him alone, I think everything would have been fine. But any time she called or tried to see him she created a major setback for us and kept him from making a commitment to marriage."

After several months, the pressure got to be too much for Cynthia. "The first time I moved out was due to the emotional trauma of feeling like I didn't belong there," she explains. "In one sense Ted was glad that he had asked me to move in and that I was there, and in another sense he was saying, 'I'm not so sure how long you'll be here.' It was heartbreaking and demeaning to feel so insecure and vulnerable. He had all of the control in the relationship. It was up to him whether I stayed or left and whether we would get married.

"I moved back into my own apartment," Cynthia recalls, noting that she took her furnishings. "Within two months I was back at Ted's, even though I was really putting myself in a bad position."

Fearful of provoking Ted into ending their relationship permanently, Cynthia had no bargaining power. She could only sit back and watch things unravel. "I couldn't stop Ted from running off to a university campus to visit his young girlfriend. In my mind, it seemed absolutely ridiculous that a grown man would be entertaining a college coed and her eighteen-year-old girlfriends. I know he was flattered by the idea, but the thought of him with all those kids was a hoot. Ted played a funny role with this girl. He was like a father, a lover, and a friend. She used to call constantly to ask for money. I don't know why. Her parents had plenty.

"My anger grew over these incidents and the limbo I found myself in. I was furious that I had put myself right back in the same precarious predicament. When I left the second time approximately six months later, it was in complete anger. The first two days after my clearing out, I didn't hear from Ted. Then he called and we would talk but not make plans to see each other. One Friday night I saw him circling my apartment in his car. We each knew it was inevitable that we would get back together."

Cynthia moved back in with Ted and into a condo they decorated together. Within a short time, Ted agreed to marry. But this on-again, off-again relationship was to continue to haunt them for several more years.

"The night before the wedding I went out with three very close women friends," continues Cynthia. "They purposely got me somewhat drunk and gave me $800 they had pulled together along with a packed bag. They took me to the airport and coaxed me into buying a ticket. They wanted me to leave and not show the next day. I purchased a ticket for Florida, but while I was waiting for the plane I thought, 'I can't do this. I'm getting married tomorrow. My parents will be in town in six hours.' I was supposed to be having the best time of my life, and I was miserable. I picked up the suitcase and took a cab home.

"When I got home, I found Ted and his college girlfriend sitting in our condo arguing whether he should or shouldn't go through with the ceremony. She knew what levers to pull on him and started the turmoil all over again. The next day as we were drove to our wedding, Ted said, 'I don't why know why I am doing this.'"

Two months after Ted and Cynthia's wedding, the perilous patterns they established while living together struck a blow to their marriage. Cynthia came home one afternoon to find that Ted had moved out. "He said he needed time to think. I knew that his college friend was behind it. She was coming home," Cynthia says. "He moved into his brother's place. He didn't know when he was coming back. He returned after several months, but when he came back, the turmoil was hardly over."

Ted left once more, this time after Cynthia turned up pregnant. "We were supposed to go away for the weekend, but when he heard I was pregnant he said I couldn't come with him. He threatened that he was leaving and wasn't coming back. It still chills me inside that he warned me, 'When I come back, I don't want you to be here. If you are, I am going to put your things in the street.'"

However, his behavior did not bother Cynthia as much as it did in the past, because she had a newfound sense of security. Instead of acquiring this from a loving, caring, and dependable mate, her security grew from knowing she was having Ted's baby. "I knew if I left I wouldn't be leaving empty-handed," she says. "I went to my parents' home and came back at the end of the weekend. Ted wasn't there. He showed up later. He realized he could not behave so erratically when there was a child involved.

"Once I was a mother, I was a different person," admits Cynthia. "Having his child was like staking a claim. No matter how much bullshit he gave me up to this point, I still got the prize. I still got a little piece of him that he couldn't take away. He could never again threaten to put my things out on the sidewalk."

It took Ted two years to settle into a domestic life that Cynthia rates near a ten after a decade of marriage. But it seems that there were still some things beyond Cynthia's control—until quite recently. For instance, when his ex-preppie suffered a major trauma in her love life several years ago, she called from out of town and asked Ted to help her. He did.

Cynthia and Ted's patterns of live-in love had dug a deep trench into the relationship. It took years to fill the void with better precedents for a happy marital union.

A Mighty Leap from Sexy Live-Ins to Committed Marriage Partners

This is the story of Garth and Sybil. They met a year and a

half after Garth's divorce. They dated and moved in together four months after they met. Having just liberated himself from a fifteen-year marriage, Garth says, "I was looking for a girlfriend whose eyes would get real big when she saw me. That was it.

"I think it is accurate to call Sybil's and my relationship in the early days of living together a sexual companionship," explains Garth. "It was an intimate relationship without a commitment. That's the way I wanted it."

Garth could hardly envision himself, forty and free, making a permanent relationship out of his romance with Sybil, twenty-three and fresh out of college. To make sure she got the point, he helped pay rent on her empty apartment for more than two years.

"I wanted a relationship where if it didn't work and we weren't happy it would be a ten-minute drive to change it," says Garth. "Sybil was devoted and in love early on. She wanted more out of the relationship. I would tell her that she was young and pretty and would ultimately marry someone else and have kids. I already had mine. I loved being a father but did not want more children.

"I could feel things progressing too far and was not ready to make any kind of commitment. After six months, I asked her to move out.

"We ran into each other a while later at a party," Garth continues. "We had this incredible passion for each other, and Sybil ended up moving back in with me. There was no change in our relationship, however. Part of the problem was it was my home, my life—not hers. Nothing was *ours*. We went through several unpleasant years full of back-stabbing, arguments, and turmoil. Somehow the passion and enjoyment of being together was always there to a degree.

"Sybil became uncomfortable living together because I would not make more of a commitment or agree to have children with her. I, on the other hand, felt closed in, like the back door was locked. There were some personal issues I needed to work out and didn't have the space to do it. I closed myself off from her. Neither one of us developed a real understanding for each other by living together.

"I wasn't ready to get married. I almost didn't. For a time before we got engaged, I was living under the threat of an ultimatum:

'Marry me or I'm leaving.' I finally said, 'I don't care how much I may care about you, I am not taking that step.' She moved out, and I tried to resist going after her, but within four weeks we were engaged."

Married now for more than three years, Garth rates his marriage no more satisfying than a two or three on a scale of one to ten. In fact, he says, "Things got progressively worse after we were married about six months. At times, I wished I had not gotten married.

"I have no problem with marriage," Garth explains. "I think the married couples in my social circle are the happiest people I know. They have worked out their problems and built strong relationships. Sybil and I didn't do that when we lived together and haven't been able to since we got married. Nothing really changed, at least nothing fundamental and deep inside of me. Our relationship was based on companionship, passion, and sex, but marriage should be based on strong commitment, caring, patience, and nurturing.

"The hardest thing in life to change are our roles. All those years Sybil was my live-in girlfriend I thought of her in one way. Now all of a sudden, in the same house with all the same circumstances surrounding us, I am supposed to look at her differently and assign her a role as my wife. You can't change this all of a sudden, just because we got married. I couldn't.

"I still have one foot in the relationship and one foot out. It is just like when we lived together. I lack a total commitment to Sybil in an emotional sense. I wanted a marriage relationship with somebody more on my same emotional and intellectual level, more grown up and experienced in life—not a roommate. But now that I'm into it, I don't want to fail. I want this relationship to work. The jury is still out as to whether or not it can. We are going for help, but progress is very slow."

Seven months ago, Sybil and Garth were separated. Today, they are back together. It appears that it is easy to rock back and forth when two feet are not firmly planted on the same side of the door.

It should be abundantly clear by now how the Living Together Trap wraps itself around and burrows deep inside the lives of so many unsuspecting men and women. There is a way to try to escape the trap. The next six chapters will reveal the avenues, questions, and actions that lead to greater success in live-in love. Setting the stage for this endeavor first requires getting to know some of the couples who experienced the best of live-in love.

CHAPTER 7

The Best of Live-In Love

If approached with caution, evaluated realistically, and nurtured thoughtfully, live-in love can be a success. Couples who are succeeding, however, did not readily appear in my randomly selected interviews but necessitated deliberate search. Men and women who demonstrate the best of live-in love:

- believe that living together benefited their relationship and provided mutual satisfaction without succumbing to the hazards revealed in previous chapters.
- affirm that under the same circumstances, they would move in with their partner again.

The most satisfied couples say they have succeeded in living together through trial and error, good sound judgment, and just plain luck.

The best cases of live-in love do not represent perfect relationships. There is no such thing. Still, these partnerships came close to fulfilling the promises of love and happiness with less risk of the heartache that prevailed among a number of women and a fewer but significant number of men who chose live-in love. It is worthwhile to pay close attention to the ingredients of these success stories.

◆　◆　◆

BASIC INGREDIENTS FOR
THE BEST OF LIVE-IN LOVE

It is a common misconception that successful cohabitation is based on one criterion: commitment. Granted, commitment is a primary factor, and the more committed one is to the relationship the better. Nevertheless, current data and a more thorough investigation of live-in relationships demonstrate that one's level of commitment is only one of the critical factors determining the outcome of living together.

Regardless of age or previous marital status, men and women who fare best with live-in love appear to join households after they develop:

- a relationship that is nurtured over time and based on trust, friendship, and love.
- a mutual readiness to participate in an intimate, exclusive relationship that has the potential to evolve into matrimony or a long-term living arrangement.
- a serious commitment to each other and their relationship.

SUCCEEDING AT LIVE-IN LOVE AFTER
MARRIAGE AND DIVORCE

Divorced men and women who receive the greatest rewards from live-in love rely less on luck, chance, or raw emotion than do their counterparts who have never been married. Divorced men and women who find living together beneficial combine their individual strengths with a keen sense of reality to chart the course of their sometimes uncertain live-in relationships.

Two factors contribute to the potential instability of living together for this population. According to Larry L. Bumpass and James A. Sweet of the University of Wisconsin and Andrew Cherlin of Johns Hopkins University, fewer divorced cohabitors expect to marry their live-in partners and therefore have a less defined future. While 60 percent of those individuals that remarried during

1980–1987 did cohabit, only 46 percent of them married the partner they lived with. A divorced man in his early forties admitted that there is no way he would remarry without trying living with a woman first. Curiosity over this growing lifestyle, not his desire to test a relationship, was the motive he gave for moving in with a woman he did not love. Second, 40 percent of the households of divorced cohabitors include the presence of at least one partner's children. These couples report more problems with their relationships than do childless cohabitors.

The two couples in this section resolved both issues—one by living together and then marrying and the other by extended, unwed cohabitation. Why they chose to live together, how they addressed the marriage issue, and how they succeeded at carving out satisfying relationships separate them from the less happy, more frequent endings to live-in love.

The Benefits of an Unshakable Sense of Independence

Julie points out two ingredients that have contributed to the success of her six-year live-in relationship with Barry:

1. Her sense of independence.
2. Her ability to avoid a rigid predisposition toward marriage.

Married at twenty-one and divorced twelve years later, Julie found that living without her husband was a relatively easy adjustment. Her highest priority then and now was creating a stable, loving home for her girls, who lived with her every other week.

Depending on Herself: A Primary Factor

Julie relates the story of her relationship with Barry, which began when she was thirty-four and he forty-two. "I was not looking for someone to take care of me," she says. "When Barry moved in, I always felt if it didn't work, he could move out. I never saw that as a potential problem for me to deal with."

Julie attributes her attitude in great part to her unshakable sense of independence developed over the years. "When I was newly

99

married to my first husband, he wanted me to become extremely independent. After a decade of marriage I think I became so independent that I didn't need or want him anymore. We had never developed real intimacy. I decided if we couldn't achieve a more meaningful relationship, one that went beyond our superficial companionship, I was leaving. That is what I did.

"Ultimately, I think I have become more independent than a lot of women I know because I don't need a lot from a man. I am good on my own and enjoy my own company. And being financially independent is a big plus. I am fortunate to have a trust fund from grandparents that supplements my income from my business and my settlement from my divorce. I have no money worries for my future or my daughters'."

Julie's viewpoint is indeed contrary to a large percentage of female cohabitors who prefer to marry and assume that it will provide greater economic and financial security.

"I was not in a big hurry to find another husband," Julie explains. "Barry and I had known each other before our divorces. We ran in the same social circles, and our children when to school together. All of that was very important to me when we started to date. I did not want to have strange men in the house the weeks the girls were living with me. In fact, I rarely went out with men unless it was a week Sally and Tess, then six and eight, were with their father.

"Barry and I were very comfortable together, and so were all of our children. My girls and his two children, a boy and a girl, were around the same ages. They would all come over for dinner or a swim and sometimes spend the night. My daughters were crazy about Barry," says Julie. "I cannot stress how important this was for me.

"Barry and I developed a very special relationship over the next two years that had the intimacy missing in my marriage; I could be myself with him. He knew me better than anyone ever had. But that wasn't all: He was romantic, caring, and generous, and he had a great sense of humor and zest for life that kept both my daughters and me up.

"The girls liked it when Barry was in the house, although I

never allowed him to stay overnight when they were there. I was not comfortable having the girls witness the fact that this was a sexual relationship. Both my ex-husband and I had been extremely protective about this. Consequently, when Barry moved in, he took the empty guest bedroom," Julie says. "That is where he still sleeps every other week when the girls are with us. He has no objections. Our relationship goes much deeper than sex.

"I had no problem with the idea of living with a man outside of marriage," Julie admits. "I had been introduced to nontraditional lifestyles from a young age. My father's business gave us the opportunity to spend extended periods of time in Sweden, where living together was commonplace, and I had lived with my husband before we married. My primary concern when Barry joined our household was not to put my daughters in an awkward position or jeopardize their friendships with children whose parents were not quite as liberal. I did not want to provoke Tess and Sally's father."

Julie and Barry worked out a comfortable and satisfying living arrangement, but it was not trouble-free. After Barry first moved in, Julie thought there might be a chance of becoming one of these combined Brady Bunch families her daughters wanted. But Julie, affirming the wisdom of her judgment at that time, says, "*I was willing to allow things to evolve. You cannot be goal-oriented when someone moves in under these circumstances.* You shouldn't be set just on marriage. Second marriages come with a lot of baggage. You need to know how that affects your life together. There were too many complications for me to marry Barry even though he wanted to. Fortunately, he was willing to continue our live-in relationship without being married."

In fact, Julie felt marrying him might wreak havoc on their loving relationship. Julie feared that Barry's children and the relationship with his ex-wife might be more problematic for her as wife and stepmother.

"Barry does not have a good rapport with his ex-wife," Julie explains. "This makes life very difficult for him, me, and his children. Barry's ex had a lover and wanted the divorce. Once she got it, she went wild, failing to properly supervise the kids or properly manage their home. I simply cannot relate to these children the way they have been raised.

"I respect Barry's children and want him to do the very best for them, but that doesn't mean indulging them to the point that it is detrimental. He gives into their every whim unconditionally, even though they may be seriously neglecting their school work or getting into all kinds of trouble. He is just as permissive with his ex-wife, who tries to sue him every two years for more money. She has an income of over $60,000 but never has food in the refrigerator or a meal on the table. Barry doesn't insist that she provide the proper home or supervision for the children. Instead he treats her the same way he does them. When his ex-wife learned that Barry and I were taking all of the children on a vacation, she sent one of the kids over to ask Barry for money so that she could take her own trip. He handed over the money without making her promise to take better care of his children."

Since Barry moved in six years ago, Julie has been determined to prevent his problems from disrupting the calm, well-structured atmosphere of her home. The best way she could do this, she feels, has been to remain unmarried.

"Staying single has meant that I don't have to be involved as much with Barry's kids. I can separate myself from the issues that could cause conflict in our relationship and in my home. I am very honest about it, and Barry is not offended by that. We don't argue over it, although we discuss his kids a lot, and I try to help out. Barry is out of town frequently on business, and I am his substitute parent, taking his children to the doctor's or giving them money they need. For a while I was even taking off work and picking up the children every day after school to make sure they got home to begin doing their homework. But before I would get home, they would be out running around. I told Barry he had to hire a sitter to be at home after school.

"But no matter how much we talk or what I suggest, the situation remains much the same. It is aggravating," Julie admits, "but I have no control over it. I tell myself it is none of my business.

"I do think that our children should come first for each of us. I would have no problem if he sought total custody of his children and moved into his own place to improve their home environment.

But I have made it clear that this is my home and his children cannot live here. We have rules in our home that his children don't understand. Neither does Barry.

"If we were married, it would be our home and I would not have the right to deny his children the opportunity to live with us. Because Barry travels for work as much as four days a week, it is entirely conceivable that I might have the sole responsibility for them on a full-time basis. I hardly think that is fair, since I share custody of my own daughters. Nor am I sure how Sally and Tess's father would feel having these relatively incorrigible teenagers live in the same house with us.

"Having them move in at this point would be emotionally and financially taxing for me, as well as disruptive for my children. I have to monitor my own mental health. At one point I was a borderline alcoholic; I was able to get control of this with help from an outpatient treatment center. I would also have to give up my studio in the house and rent one, which would cost me over $8,000 a year. Protecting my inheritance is another consideration. Barry's ex has tried to sue me for money. I don't want any financial entanglements.

"There are simply too many issues in the way of marriage," Julie says matter-of-factly.

Julie is definitely protecting her hearth, home, and heart and is realistic enough to admit, "If we were married, I would put more demands on Barry. I would probably be more possessive of his time and even expect him to spend more of his money on me. I might not be so understanding of his generosity to his ex-wife and all of the thousands of extra dollars he spends on his children. Right now, we both share our living expenses, and I take care of myself and the girls. Without us being man and wife, his finances are his own business.

"I feel more freedom to do as I please by living together, and it enables me to be more accepting and tolerant of the situation. It keeps me concentrating on the positives and not the negatives, which is essential in any relationship.

"I don't know if there is a need to get married anyway. Barry and I both feel very secure in our relationship and treat each other with respect and consideration. He is a lover, a roommate, and a good friend without being my husband. I can honestly see this relationship going on forever. I am happier than I have ever been," concludes Julie.

Sam and Cindy, Heading in the Same Direction

Cindy and Sam each pinpoint a special ingredient that contributed to their successful live-in relationship.

He says: A mutual understanding of the seriousness of the relationship.
She says: Self-esteem.

Their meeting may have been serendipitous, but developing a lifetime love affair was not. Sam and Cindy, forty-five and thirty-six at the time, literally bumped into each other at a cocktail party. From there it didn't take long for Cindy's sweet manner and Sam's immediate interest to motivate the two to continue the evening over dinner.

Forgetting the Past and Forging a Future

Before Cindy met Sam on that fateful night, Cindy had already called a halt to her mismatched marriage five years earlier. Then she jumped into a one-year abusive affair that ended when her lover's aggressive physical behavior landed her in a hospital emergency room. That's when Cindy determined to change the course of her life.

"The way I had allowed people to treat me in the past was symptomatic of my low self-esteem," Cindy explains. "I started searching for my inner self and realized through the help of a support group that I was a pretty decent person. The other women in the group helped me to see that there was no reason I had to allow a man or a woman to take advantage of me. By the time I met Sam, I could relate to him in a much healthier way."

Her newfound strength was readily apparent. "Cindy's self-esteem was always high. It's the whole reason our relationship worked," Sam reports.

To make it succeed there were a number of high hurdles to jump.

For one, Sam lived with his wife and youngest child when he and Cindy met. Unhappy for years, Sam had every intention of someday divorcing the woman he had married when she was a pregnant school girl and he was eighteen. For a good part of their marriage he sought sexual satisfaction and soothing emotional support from extramarital affairs. He gained personal gratification from finishing college, supporting three children, and becoming a wealthy businessman.

"I wasn't happy about the fact that Sam was married," reveals Cindy, "but I truly believed in a spiritual sense he was sent to me. He was just what I had ordered, and I was just what he had been looking for. There was an immediate attraction between us, and I fell head over heels in love with him. We were so in tune with each other that I knew Sam had to be sincere. We both knew what we were feeling for each other was special."

It was the kind of love some of the men and women in previous chapters were searching for, but it did not give Sam the license to take advantage of Cindy in any way. She was full of self-confidence and was able to manage the relationship, taking into full account what was best for her.

"Within months of beginning our relationship, we were on vacation and sitting at a very noisy bar," Cindy recalls. "I asked Sam, 'Now that you have me, what are you going to do with me?' I didn't know that he hadn't heard my question. I thought he just refused to answer. I said, 'I will not be your mistress; I will not be trifled with,' and ran out of the bar crying. Sam ran after me. When he understood what had provoked my fury, he assured me that he took our relationship seriously.

"For the first year of our affair, Sam kept saying he was going to leave his wife. I believed him, but it worried me," Cindy admits. "I think I had set a deadline in my head for him to prove it. When after a year I didn't see any signs that he was actually getting ready to leave, I became very businesslike one day when he came over to see me. He wanted to know what was wrong. I said, 'You were going to leave her, and nothing has happened. If I don't see any signs soon, I will not be able to continue in this relationship.'"

Cindy's words spurred Sam to action. He saw his attorney immediately and told his wife he was filing for divorce. As it turns out, she was not oblivious to his affair. In fact, she told him he could stay in the house and keep his lover. He declined the offer.

When Sam moved out, Cindy did not move in, despite Sam's persistent invitation. Concerned about the welfare of her two pre-teenage sons, fearful of her ex-husband's reaction, and confused about how she was going to manage to keep everybody happy, Cindy was not sure if moving in would be good for her and Sam. "I am a pleaser and a fixer," she says, "but after another six months I decided it was time to do what I wanted. I want to live with Sam. I thought if I was happy, the kids would be happy, too."

"When we decided to move in together," Sam notes, "there was no question but that we would be with each other for the rest of our lives and most likely get married unless something went horribly wrong. I knew that Cindy wanted to be married, and I knew that there would be a time when the matter would come to a head. I would either have to marry her or she would leave."

"Living together was a good solution for us, for what we were striving for at that time in our lives. I truly thought it would lead to marriage," Cindy agrees, "but the timing had to be right."

Her assessment was correct.

"I was gun-shy," Sam admits. "I had just come out of a brutal divorce that cost me a ton of money. I was not ready to get married again that easily. I needed to prove to myself that I could have a good relationship with a woman."

There were definitely matters of adjustment once Cindy, Sam, and her two boys settled in together. For one thing, Cindy began to feel herself slipping back into old patterns.

"A friend told me that I was losing my sparkle. I stopped and examined what was happening. I realized I was giving up my power and self-esteem again by agreeing with Sam and doing so many little things I didn't really want to. I had to quit being the martyr and stand up for myself. I needed to do what was best for me. What was best for me had to be best for our relationship."

What was best for Cindy entailed letting Sam know that she was not to be taken for granted. When he got up one sunny Saturday morning and announced without any previous notice that he was golfing for the day, she said, "Well what about me?" It wasn't that she did not approve of his outing but rather that he had failed to inform her earlier of his plans. "I could have made arrangements to be with some of my friends that Sam didn't care to spend time with," she says. "If I didn't speak up, he could have easily misconstrued that I agreed with his actions."

Sam was willing to learn how to be a more considerate partner. "I was willing to change to some degree and make some concessions for Cindy," Sam says. "It was obvious how willing she was to change, too. It just made sense to meet her halfway and really try to do the small things that were important to her. One day when we were taking a walk, she put her arms around me. I was uncomfortable and moved away slightly. She took my hand and said, 'You have to hold on to me. It is so important to me.' I said, 'Well, okay, then I'll try.' We have gone for therapy intermittently to improve our communication. This was new to me. My wife was vicious at best and our interaction limited."

Sam began to sense that Cindy's timetable was running out after about a year and a half of living together. He knew if he did not propose soon, he might lose her. Still there was one more item that needed to be resolved while they were living together.

"Cindy had to be dragged kicking and screaming into the real world," Sam explains. "She had this image of a big happy family with me taking over the role of father. It took me a long time to convince her it wasn't going to be that way. I would be her sons' friend, but I wasn't going to be their father. I had been parenting since I was eighteen. I had done it all already—pre-teen, teen, and post-teen. I told her that I would help support her, but that they were her children and her responsibility. Financially, I would treat them as I have my own, but that was all I could offer. I was firm on this one."

"I had to come to terms that I had gone from being a single parent with children to a single parent with a live-in relationship," Cindy says, her voice filled with resignation and disappointment.

"Sam was not going to become their father. I had to learn that this wasn't an issue for the children. It wasn't an issue for Sam. It was my own issue. I wanted life to be a version of 'Father Knows Best.' I had to accept that it would never be that way."

Not all of Cindy's dreams have come true, but the essentials are there. "I wanted to be married," acknowledges Cindy, "and I wanted someone who adored me as much as I adored him. Sam still adores me. He still wraps himself around me at night and calls several times a day. Despite our differences, we both want our relationship to work. We'll always work hard at it."

LIVE-IN LOVE WITHOUT THE EXPERIENCE OF MARRIAGE

Recent studies indicate that more than 80 percent of the young men and women who live together and have never been married either intend to marry their live-in partner or think they will. Not all of them do. Being successful at live-in love for this group is largely based on their relationship culminating in matrimony. At the same time, however, these couples lack experience or a clear vision of what a committed relationship entails, whether it be living together or marriage. Consequently, luck plays a part in determining the success or failure of the live-in relationship. That is not to say success is based solely on happenstance.

Two couples demonstrate how to minimize the element of luck and maximize the potential for success.

Taking the Luck out of Live-In Love

If matrimony is the ultimate goal, there is less risk of heartache and disappointment for couples who:

- possess all of the basic ingredients for the best of live-in love.
- get to know each other well before moving in.
- set a wedding date prior to moving in.
- demonstrate respect for their partner and their relationship.
- develop their relationship step by step.

- do not take living together lightly.
- are the marrying kind.
- believe marriage is forever.
- use living together as a transition period.

These critical factors, plus attitudes expressed by couples like those we are about to meet, help to ensure the success of living together. Young men are generally more resistant to marriage than young women and are particularly anxious about giving up the freedom of being single. Understanding women like Amy and Nancy provides a reassuring atmosphere and affords the time to waylay those fears and adjust to the type of commitment required for lifelong relationship.

Jordan and Amy

Family members fixed up Jordan and Amy on a blind date when they were twenty-four and twenty-one, respectively. They hit it off real well and spent hours talking about the loss of a parent, an experience they both suffered while in high school. They dated for three months before sleeping with each other, and Jordan reports it was different from any other sexual encounter.

"Amy was the first woman I wanted to spend the night with. After that first time, I didn't sleep with anyone else," Jordan admits. "We started talking about living together after about five months, but Amy did not move in with me for two years. When she did move in, we had set a secret wedding date for nine months later.

"I did not want to rush things," he says. "I had to allow the relationship to grow naturally. I couldn't force it, and I wouldn't allow someone to move in unless I was really serious. I wanted to make sure that Amy was the right woman for me. I had to struggle with the idea that no one is perfect. I would go through periods of doubt when I would step back and reflect on what I really wanted. I needed time to digest what was happening to me. It was important for me to feel that I was being cautious. My brother had just gotten divorced, and I did not want to end up the same way.

"I was perfectly honest with Amy. I let her know how I was feeling, but she knows me better than I know myself. When she did move in, I had every intention of marrying her. We stuck by the wedding date she had set, but I wouldn't have minded waiting another year or two. Living together and getting married was a big transition for me, but I was prepared to make the concessions I thought I should.

"When I would be out with the guys, I came home even when I didn't really want to. I didn't think it was right for Amy to be sitting home alone, even if she kept telling me it was okay."

"Jordan is a very unselfish person," says Amy. "When we moved in together, he felt like he had a certain responsibility to me. I always felt secure in our relationship because he is such a good person. I didn't have to pressure him about anything. I think we have something that is unique."

Married for a year now, Amy and Jordon seem to have little to worry about in this marriage. Artful and prudent secrets explored in my book *Marriage Secrets: How to Have a Lifetime Love Affair* may help to keep their love and good intentions on track. Jordan is prepared to settle in for good. "I enjoy having Amy with me and look forward to the next fifty years together."

Jeffrey and Elizabeth

Jeffrey and Elizabeth were acquaintances before they started dating when she was twenty-five and he was twenty-two. Once Elizabeth fell in love with Jeffrey, she knew that she would have to be patient and allow him to grow up and mature a little more before moving on to a committed relationship. At one point they even broke up, but according to Jeffrey, "It just wasn't any good without her. I knew that I loved her; I didn't know if it was the kind of love that would take you through a whole married life. Even though I wasn't ready to get married yet, I got engaged. I wanted to because I loved making Elizabeth happy. I have always been sensitive to the way she was feeling."

When they moved in after dating a few years, they were engaged with a wedding date set ten months later. Elizabeth wasn't all that keen on living together but had promised Jeffrey she would once the ring was on her finger.

"I knew that my parents thought it was wrong to live together," Elizabeth reveals. "My sister graduated college and moved in with her boyfriend, and then they broke up. Her boyfriend said he wanted to date around. My sister was pushing hard to get married, but I knew they wouldn't. They really didn't love each other and really weren't making a future together. When I looked at them compared with Jeff and me, they seemed like roommates. I think being engaged was really important and made all the difference. We had already made a commitment to each other. Jeffrey is such a good person that I never doubted his intentions. I always trust him and feel so lucky to have someone like him.

"Living together turned out to be a wise decision for us," Elizabeth explains. "It gave Jeffrey the time to rid himself of some lingering doubts about married life. I think it's why marriage wasn't such a big adjustment. Moving in together was the big adjustment."

"I knew that when I took my marriage vows it meant that I couldn't be with other women," Jeffrey admits. "I wasn't sure if I could really do that. And I wasn't sure if I was ready to give up all of my freedom. The funny thing is, I am really a homebody and realized that shortly after Elizabeth moved in. I liked the way she helped get my house in shape, buying carpet and putting up curtains. If I had to choose between being with her or with the guys, it would be her. It wasn't even a big deal calling and letting her know if I was going to be late getting home. We treated each other with respect and consideration. I liked getting ready to go to parties and being a couple. Living together did not make me love her any less."

Part of this success story should be attributed to Elizabeth, who knew what she had to do to make the transition period work. "There was a point when I really believe Jeffrey was thinking he couldn't go through with this. So I knew it was up to me to fit in. One thing I wanted to do was make his house look like a married couple's home instead of a frat house," says Elizabeth. "I moved my things in and put all of his frat house paraphernalia, like bar mirrors and stuff, in one room. I called it his Identity Room. He got excited about it. I forced myself into being the lady of the house.

"I also knew I had to get rid of all of his buddies who kept hanging around," continues Elizabeth. "We have a hot tub in the back and they would come over and then just come on in. One day I came home and found them watching TV and drinking beer. I started running the sweeper, and I think they got the hint. Then I began locking the doors so they couldn't just walk in.

"By the time we got married, I think Jeffrey was really ready, and so was I. I knew that I belonged here with him and that he had gotten the freedom of running around with his friends out of his system. Now when I come home he is waiting to do things with me. He always tells people how happy he is; that makes me feel good. He is so understanding and supportive. I feel like I am a better person because of him."

"Today, Elizabeth is the most important thing in my life," Jeffrey says in his soft-spoken, gentle manner. "We have been married three years, and I never in a million years thought marriage would be this great. I can't believe how happy I am, even if Elizabeth maneuvered me into it."

Jimmy and Nancy

Half of the couples who cohabit in the United States either break up or marry within the first year and a half living together, according to Larry L. Bumpers and James A. Sweet of the University of Wisconsin. Jimmy and Nancy are among the other 50 percent. They dated for two years before moving in together with a moderate amount of commitment to their relationship. Under the standards of the exploration in this book, the first four years they spent together would easily fit under the heading "Risky Business for Women." The last ten years exemplify the best of live-in love. The distinct differences between the early and later years form a handy, instructive comparison to keep in mind.

When Nancy moved in at the age of twenty-three, she says, "I wasn't thinking long-term. Jimmy and I had had a relationship for about six months in college, but it ended when he graduated and went to Europe. Before we hooked up again after I graduated from college he lived with another woman for two years, which left him noticeably leery of women and relationships. When we did get together, Jimmy treated me much the same way as he did when we were coeds.

"He would pursue me in lots of ways," Nancy explains. "By the time I would decide I was ready for a more serious relationship, he would pull back. For the first couple of years we knew each other, we were constantly on different wavelengths. When I felt him withdraw again, I became fearful that if I fell in love with him and let him know, he would cool off completely. I was definitely protecting myself and continued to think this way even when we moved in together, although I felt that there were signs that he loved me. I didn't stop feeling this way until we had lived together for several years."

Nancy and Jimmy's early years together were tentative and did not incorporate the type of commitment exhibited by other lovers in this chapter. Neither Nancy nor Jimmy were at a point to pledge themselves fully to one another. Cognizant of her needs and Jimmy's, Nancy felt living together initially enabled them to be together without suffocating the freedom each required to continue their individual exploration of themselves.

"Our relationship was built on more than a casual sexual relationship. We were more like kindred spirits, and I had a real feeling that this could eventually develop into a serious relationship. I was really interested in this guy and I had a certain amount of love and affection for him. There was a general understanding between us that we would grow together and share interesting things together. That dimension has always been important to both of us. But at the same time, there were no guarantees that either of us wouldn't fall in love with someone else during this period or that Jimmy might not want to take off and resume his vagabond lifestyle. Maybe this attitude was part of my defense mechanism, but I think it was practical to realize that either one of us could have become enamored with someone or something else at that time."

Nancy admits she was taking a chance moving in with Jimmy then: "I can't emphasize enough how lucky I was—lucky that I landed with him instead of someone else with less character. He is extremely ethical and has a moral streak a mile wide. I probably should have asked myself if what I was doing was risky, but it was and is my feeling that living together is a good way to test a relationship—so why put it off? I wanted to spend time with Jimmy. I liked his companionship."

Beliefs are one thing; emotions are another. While Nancy may have been more willing than other women to accept the uncertainty in her relationship and understand the roots of it, there nonetheless came a point when she said, "'I don't know if I can stand anymore of Jimmy's vacillating. It keeps me on the edge not knowing if we will dissolve our relationship tomorrow.' It was almost two and a half years that we had been together when the whole thing culminated in a scene. We were at our lowest ebb. I actually dated other men at that time but never told him about it. It felt good to feel attractive to them.

"Jimmy was so agitated during this period, and I didn't know if it was because he wanted to go out with other people, take off and travel, or was having difficulty making important career decisions. He had become so preoccupied with his own feelings that he was taking me for granted. I started bringing it up partly so that I could help him deal with it and partly because I didn't want to feel as if I was keeping him in a situation that was not making him happy. The conversation lasted over a few days until I started a scene, crying and making it clear I might walk. I actually thought that maybe we would break up."

However, baring her soul rather than keeping herself in check as she had been doing proved to be to her advantage. "It turned out," recalls Nancy, "that Jimmy started crying, too. He said he couldn't imagine being without me. Although it was not my intention, it apparently shook Jimmy into the realization that if I left it would be a significant loss for him.

"We were both able to relax in the relationship after we understood that each of us was committed to the other. It allowed the best and richest parts of me to surface. Previously my emotions were choked and concealed inside of me for fear that I would reveal them and scare Jimmy away.

"Once Jimmy was able to define our relationship and himself in a new way, we were able to begin talking cautiously and slowly about being with each other for a lifetime. I didn't want to think in terms of a partnership unless it was true," Nancy admits hesitantly. "When we considered each other as partners, we could think in terms of building a future together." This sounds like the turning point when Nancy and Jimmy took on the hue of the best of live-in lovers.

"The whole issue of marriage was always a non-issue. I made a very conscious choice not to consider marriage. I wanted someone to be with me out of choice, not out of volition. I thought living together was a better way for me to go about a romantic relationship. It would keep me from taking Jimmy for granted and from falling into a rut. It required energy and patience to listen to Jimmy attentively and be alert to what he was saying. I wanted to sort of keep my standards high. Jimmy might have even found it appealing that I was different from other women and did not want to get married. But this was not my strategy for playing games but for living my life and keeping myself interesting.

"I demanded this of myself, and I expected no less from Jimmy. I expected him to help me grow and to introduce me to new things, to be kind of heart, and to help guide me to be all I could be. If being with him couldn't do that, then I didn't want to be with him. Granted, some of my ideas on marriage may have grown out of my parents' unhappy marriage, but I think they also stem from a certain amount of self-confidence and pride that made me decide I would not want a man to hang around because of a marriage certificate," Nancy explains.

However, four months ago after being live-in partners for fourteen years, Jimmy and Nancy got married. "I was pregnant but subsequently miscarried," Nancy says. "Jimmy thought it would be easier for us to be married. I don't really feel that I betrayed my principles. Ninety-five percent of me says it doesn't matter anymore if we live together or are married. Either way—marriage or living together—this relationship has afforded us the opportunity to be each other, to experience companionship, ready support, all the wonders of a warm body next to you, and to escape the loneliness that is at everybody's door."

THE OTHER SIDE OF LUCK

Putting luck aside and succeeding at live-in relationships, even for those with the best odds, requires thoughtful, cautious action. In order to join the ranks of the best of live-in love, begin by considering the questions and advice offered in Chapter 8.

CHAPTER 8

Programming for Success

Ready for a new beginning, a fresh start?

Cynthia, thirty-five years of age, suffered two failed attempts at live-in love. "Unfortunately, you have to take the romance out of the situation and tear it apart pragmatically," she says. "It may burst your bubble, but otherwise your eyes are closed and you may not know what you are doing."

To achieve a better track record than Cynthia's, consider this approach to increase your power and control over your destiny. Don't balk at the notion that relationships need analyzing or managing. Even the most successful long-term partnerships require tending. Pertinent issues and penetrating questions that help steer live-in lovers away from trouble and toward a more fruitful relationship are addressed in this chapter. Both sexes should feel empowered to act decisively and in their own best interest when considering the advice and suggestions from experienced live-ins.

PLAYING TWENTY QUESTIONS

Playing twenty questions is the first step toward taking charge of live-in love. These probing queries devised by experienced live-ins are designed to be asked prior to moving in together to prevent making that blind purchase. However, if you are already living with someone, don't turn the page quickly. This is a handy exercise for the wise man or woman who wishes to scout for the strengths, weaknesses, and potential trouble spots in a relationship.

This line of questioning has the tendency to make lovers uncomfortable. For instance, when a woman whose relationship flashed danger to a more objective eye was asked, "Are you completely comfortable with your live-in arrangement?" she answered, "I am until people ask me questions like this."

If this makes you uneasy, perhaps this is a sign that something is awry. It may be tempting to proceed in a cavalier and self-protective manner, denying the seriousness of the questions. Don't try to fool yourself. *To program for success, it is imperative that one maintain absolute honesty while proceeding through this chapter.* Because live-in love often vacillates between extreme highs and lows, it is beneficial to write down your responses to these twenty questions and date them. They may be a worthwhile point of reference at a later date.

Going for a Consensus

1. What is my motivation for moving in? Is my intended live-in's motivation the same as mine?

It shouldn't be too difficult to assess your own motivation if you are honest with yourself. It might be more difficult to assess your lover's. Don't assume anything. Ask your partner what he or she wants out of the live-in arrangement.

Brenda warns, "We didn't talk about what moving in actually meant. I wish we had. The most important thing at the time was figuring out the finances. Maybe you don't ask more important questions because it is scary and things move quickly."

Until you are certain about the motives on both side of the fence, avoid moving in at all costs. Drop the issue completely if you do not agree about what moving in means to you. This is fundamental to safeguarding your feelings and reducing the risk of encountering the trap, whether the live-in relationship is perceived as serious, frivolous, or primarily sexual.

There is absolutely no substitute for coming to a consensus on this one!

2. Are you equally committed to one another and to the relationship?

The answer should be "yes" or pretty close to it. The problem, Scott cautions, is "Women don't listen to men. They hear what they want to and then are surprised when they learn he isn't as committed as she when they move in."

What should a woman be listening for? According to Warren Farrell, Ph.D., author of *Why Men Are the Way They Are,* women should listen for sounds of love. Men, he argues, commit to a woman and to a relationship more slowly, but when they do it is out of love. Men are driven by their primary need for intimacy, respect, and appreciation—all of which form the essence of the love relationship.

Moving In with a Known Commodity

3. How well do I know my potential live-in?

Answering this question should take time and a lot of paper. What you know should not only be plentiful but also well-supported. For instance, write down simple things like where he was born, how old he is, where his parents live, if he has an ex-wife and children, if he is up-to-date on his child-support payments, if he treats his family fairly, where he went to school, where he has worked, where he has lived, what his goals and his ambitions are, who his friends are, how he gets along with people at work, and if he is in debt.

The hard part is asking yourself *how* you know all of the answers. If he says he has a great relationship with his ex, have you ever met her? If he is supposed to have this terrific job, have you ever seen his office or met his coworkers? And if he says he is in love with you, how does he show it?

4. What don't I know about my potential live-in?

This may sound like an unnecessary exercise, but pay attention to what happened to Frank and to Patrick. Frank allowed Ruth to move in two months after they met. What he didn't know was that Ruth was an alcoholic whose lifestyle would wreak havoc on his peace and tranquillity. Patrick was curious but never asked Lana, who wiggled her way into his home in just a few months, how she managed to drive such an expensive sports car and purchase such extravagant clothes on her modest income. When he decided he wanted her to move out, he realized that he must not have been the first guy to pay her a considerable amount of ready cash just to vacate the premises.

When a man or woman becomes romantically involved, there is a tendency to avoid practical issues and truths that may upset the passion of the moment. But that is precisely when one needs to be the most questioning no matter how awkward it feels and especially if moving in is a possibility. The more emotionally vested you become, the harder it is to be objective. Don't try to piece together your own explanation of your lover's inexplicable behavior. If your own line of questioning doesn't produce satisfying answers, how about a private investigator? In some areas a background check costs no more than $50. One professional California private eye reported that assignments from single men and women have increased significantly during the last few years. If you have a hunch that something in his or her story just doesn't seem to fit, trust your own intuition. According to this private eye, "women's intuition" is right 99 percent of the time.

5. Should I get to know my potential live-in better?
Absolutely! How could it possibly hurt?

According to a poll reported in a popular magazine in 1992, American men lie more than women. They tell 150 lies a week, many of which are served up to women during the initial stages of a relationship in order to promote themselves. According to Steve Carter, co-author of *What Smart Women Know,* both sexes ought to beware. Men and women both make a practice of lying to one another about themselves.

"So why hurry into it?" Peggy asks. "The only way to make sure he isn't your fantasy is to go slowly. Time has a way of putting things in a better perspective."

That's good, sound advice that should suffice.

6. Does he or she possess qualities that contribute to a good potential live-in partner?

Look for qualities found in the men and women who comprised the best of live-in love. Begin to compare your love interest against this checklist of admirable qualities:

+ honesty and integrity
+ respect for the opposite sex and for love relationships
+ ability to be loyal and faithful
+ independence
+ self-confidence
+ giving
+ support
+ maturity
+ responsibility
+ capacity for emotional intimacy
+ interesting
+ willingness to compromise
+ interest in working on a relationship.

Don't hesitate to add your own requirements to the list. Be sure you tally up enough checkmarks to make moving in a worthwhile investment.

Assessing Your Own Position

7. Do I have enough self-esteem to be able to wisely and effectively manage a love relationship?

Without self-esteem, there are three potential problems related to moving in:

a. It is tempting to move in for the wrong reasons. Lovers without self-esteem are likely to miscalculate that living together will protect a weak love interest and add security to their relationship, safeguarding their lover from others, and ensuring they will stick around.

b. Lovers make only a timid attempt to direct the course of a living-together relationship. The vast majority of women interviewed who described themselves as having high self-esteem were less likely to find themselves trapped by live-in love. This is no coincidence. Nearly every self-help book confirms that in any type of relationship, personal or business, an individual needs self-esteem to interact effectively with others. And being empowered by self-esteem to achieve a lifelong love affair is at the core of my findings on satisfying marital relationships.

c. Without self-esteem and the belief that you are a worthy partner, it is difficult at best to protect your own interests, seek an equitable partner, and tell your partner to stop stepping on your toes or to get lost.

This may be harder for women.

Stan, a New York lawyer, was not trying to be chauvinistic or conceited when he told me, "The reality is that men and women do not yet have the same status. For instance, being a single man in my thirties with a law degree and the ability to earn a fair income earns me the title of 'good catch' for women. If I am patient, I can come up with a desirable mate. A woman in the same position and same age is already considering settling for something less in a partner."

Liza, age thirty-three and full of self-esteem, agrees entirely. "I think each woman has to say to herself, 'If I never get married and have a family, I will be happy.' It takes away the sense of urgency that causes you to put yourself in precarious and unfair circumstances with men. I think the media have helped to create the hysteria many of my friends express in finding a husband. This makes them feel bad about themselves."

That is precisely the message Susan Faludi conveys with a great deal of evidence in her book *Backlash*. If you are experiencing this feeling of panic, don't pack an overnight bag—and certainly not your entire wardrobe. And don't consider moving in until your self-esteem is in full bloom. If you need to infuse yourself with a quick dose of self-esteem, begin doing what Carolyn Hillman, author of *Recovery of Your Self-Esteem,* suggests. View yourself with compassion, acceptance, respect, and encouragement. Stroke and support yourself.

And while you're at it, be your own best friend and advocate. If you don't feel you are worth all of this, you need more help in this area. Don't delay. Get it!

8. Do I need my potential live-in to make myself feel complete?

If the answer is yes, you need more time on your own. Barbara DeAngelis, Ph.D., author of *Are You the One for Me?*, cautions against becoming involved just to fill an emotional or spiritual void. It is the wrong foundation for a love relationship and a dangerous base for a live-in partnership.

The most satisfying partnerships consist of individuals who can stand independently of one another. Needing another person to complete oneself engenders an unhealthy dependence and puts one in a prime position to be taken advantage of. Not only does this place a significant burden on the relationship but relegates one partner to an inequitable position. It is hardly a posture that allows one to foster a healthy, mutual, and equitable interdependence.

9. Am I ready to make the necessary concessions?

It is virtually impossible to move in without making some concessions, even if the mutually agreed upon arrangement is no more than a casual sexual fling. One must take into consideration the most elementary issues: Are you willing to share your space and give up your privacy?

A surprising number of young women who tasted live-in relationships felt they made too many concessions. They regretted forgoing the experience of an independent living experience before moving in. They believe if they had the confidence that they could indeed make it on their own, they would not have compromised so readily and so often at their own expense. In fact, some women admit living alone might not only have altered their decision to move in but speeded the decision to move out.

Examining the Consequences

Questions 10 through 13 are simple but invaluable queries posed by live-in lovers. They challenge the would-be cohabitors to contemplate how they might handle potential perils that could arise from moving in. The safest answer to all four questions is a bold "yes." Without this level of certainty, live-in love could catch you in its trap.

10. If you are prepared to move in, are you prepared to move out?
Before you answer, take a moment to recall the testimony of the men and women who described how difficult it was to cross back over the threshold.

11. If you both agree marriage is your goal, are you sure enough of your feelings to marry this person tomorrow?
The author of this one suggests that the only appropriate answer is yes. But then someone might ask, "Why don't you just get married?" Do you have a reason, valid or otherwise?

12. Do you care enough about your potential live-in partner to accept the possibility that you might live with this person ten to twenty years and not get married?
It could happen, and it does!

13. Do you stand to gain more than you might lose if you move in?
To double-check yourself on this one, take two separate pieces of paper. On one list all the ways you can possibly benefit. On the other, with just as much vigor, list all you stand to lose. The results should be a pretty good indication of whether you should delay making a decision to move in until you evaluate the relationship.

Evaluating the Relationship

Living with a lover can be great fun. One young woman told me she loved sitting on the bed taking all night with her live-in partner. It was reminiscent of her youthful pajama parties with the girls. She did not like it quite as much, however, when he determined it was time to break up and go home to his own bedroom.

Before you move in, look closely at your relationship. Not every romance is worth the time, emotional investment, or personal sacrifices that living together requires.

◆　◆　◆

14. Is this a good relationship?

If the relationship is based on lust, assume it is temporary and don't waste your energy moving in.

To determine if your relationship is a good one with enduring qualities, see how many of the following characteristics describe it:

+ love
+ friendship
+ mutual understanding
+ empathy
+ respect
+ passion.

Then ask yourself:

+ Does the relationship bring out the very best in each one of you?
+ Does it allow you to be honest with each other?
+ Does it enable you to be yourself?
+ Are you choosing to be together out of love and not need?

If your relationship has all of these qualities and your answers to the above four questions are "yes," there is a greater chance that you will succeed at live-in love.

15. Is this an equitable relationship?

Only an affirmative response is acceptable here.

Neither partner should ever have a greater say in the decision-making process. Neither partner should ever have to make significantly more concessions or sacrifices. Neither partner should ever feel intimidated by or less important than the love interest. Neither person should ever assume control over the other's destiny.

Inequity in a relationship usurps one individual of the power that keeps both parties protected, safe, secure, and satisfied.

Claire has something to contribute on the issue of equity. She was thirty-five with two children underfoot and a dismal set of financial circumstances when William moved in. "Financially there was no way that I could keep up with William's lifestyle when he moved in. It made me uncomfortable to have such a disparity in our financial resources. I made sacrifices and gave in to him more than I think I would today because I felt indebted after borrowing money from him."

Debbie put herself into Brent's hands when they moved in together. She believed that his judgment was better than hers. He mapped out her self-improvement plan from fiscal responsibility to weight loss and gained immeasurable control over her. Curiously, his finances were in worse shape than hers and his job history dismal by comparison. Nonetheless, his fancy talk landed him in the seat of power with an improved standard of living and a six-month free ride.

16. Do you think your relationship will work if you move in together?

If you have any doubts, stay in your own home.

"I knew I was fooling myself when I moved in with Rick," Madeline admits. "I was saying one thing and doing another. If I really thought we were going to get along and eventually get married, which is what I wanted, why did we keep two dining room sets, two couches, two of everything?

"We had dated a year and a half when Rick was transferred out of town. We were both twenty-five years old and at a stage in our relationship where it was time to either get married or break up. There were a lot of reasons why I knew marriage wouldn't work for us: we had different lifestyles, came from different backgrounds, and felt strongly about our own religions. And neither of us was madly in love. I followed him anyway and moved in. All it did was perpetuate a relationship that had become a habit.

"We lived together for nine months until Rick was transferred again. When he asked me to move with him again, I told him only as his wife. He didn't propose, so I stayed behind and was glad that I had kept my couch and dining room set."

◆　◆　◆

Going in the Direction of Success

There are still four pertinent questions to ask before completing your exercise.

17. Do you think living together will benefit your relationship?

See if you can come up with at least five good reasons why you think moving in will benefit your relationship. You might want to ask your lover to do the same and compare the answers. There has been ample evidence in the previous chapters to forewarn you of the pros and cons, the probabilities, and the realities of live-in love. Why take the risk unless there is a promise of ample rewards?

18. Are your heart and mind in agreement?

Twenty-five-year-old Helen suggests that before you make a decision about moving in, ask yourself if your heart and your mind are in agreement. "It is a good test of your judgment," she thinks. "If emotionally and intellectually you think you ought to move in, chances are it is the right thing for you to do."

If heart and mind tell different stories, heed the warning.

19. Is moving in what you really want?

This question applies equally to men and women. Stop, look, listen, and think before you answer.

20. Are you willing to take a chance on live-in love?

No one can erase all the risks of live-in love. By now you should be an alert buyer. If you do decide to take the chance, consider these do's and don'ts.

You will notice that a majority of the following suggestions refer to women. That is no accident. Although we have looked at numerous relationships in which men get caught in the living together trap, women undoubtedly face the greater risk.

◆   ◆   ◆

DO'S

1. Spell out your bargain, make sure it is good for both of you, and stick to it!

Kelly says, "I didn't know when Chuck and I moved in together after dating a few months that he did not have the ability to help pay the rent. I was paying $670 living on my own and thought my share would be $300 less when we split the $940 the new apartment was going to cost us. Instead, I ended up paying the whole nut myself for the first six months. In fact, I was entirely supporting us. I should have left. It was awful and not at all what I expected. We were having fun, but it was at my expense."

If Kelly wanted to foot the bill, that was her prerogative. However, she should have been in a position to make the choice freely before moving in.

In another case, while Sandra was thrilled when Billy moved in, she was never quite happy with the bargain they struck. Billy reasoned that because Sandra owned the house, she benefited the most from his rental payment. Consequently, he felt it was unfair for him to split the monthly payment. Forget the fact that even this amount was less than he was paying for a smaller apartment. Sandra acquiesced and on top of it signed an informal agreement that Billy insisted on. It stated that if they broke up, he got a certain percentage of his rent back.

When they did call it quits, Sandra was fortunate Billy didn't try to collect on their agreement.

Men seem to get stuck in a different way. I spoke with a number of them who paid tens of thousands of dollars to end a live-in affair. How and when both men and women should protect themselves when moving in will be thoroughly examined in Chapter 11.

In the meantime, your agreement should include all money matters, including housekeeping chores and everything in between. Whether you decide to take joint or individual responsibility for these matters is best decided in advance. Sit and quietly work this out together. The entire process may tell you something about your intended. If you can't agree on these issues before you move in, what makes you think they will suddenly resolve themselves when you share the same abode?

2. Establish an etiquette for living together.

Using good etiquette demonstrates a certain level of consideration that is a good trait to develop in a live-in lover. However, be careful. If leaving the toilet seat up or not rinsing the dishes becomes a focal point for conflict, there are more significant sore spots.

Rarely did the couples who were the most committed or serious about their relationships bring up items relating to etiquette. When asked if living together helped them adjust to their partner's personal habits, they may have responded affirmatively but minimized the importance. These were petty considerations, they noted. Putting the top back on the toothpaste and not picking up clothes were hardly the kind of revelations that tested their compatibility or love. The men and women who did mention these considerations appear to be less certain about the future of their live-in relationship.

Nevertheless, there is no harm—and probably there is some good—in establishing an etiquette for living together. Anything that reduces conflict in a relationship is valuable. Here is a "Starter Set for Live-In Etiquette":

* Inform each other of your daily schedule. If you won't be home for dinner, make that clear before the soup is simmering on the stove.
* Call if you will be late getting home. Your partner may worry.
* Pick up your own dirty clothes and wet towels. A live-in partner should not be your personal housekeeper.
* Say "thank you" for a good deed and "please" when asking for favors. Live-ins should not be taken for granted.
* Be polite to each other's friends when they call. Remember two people share your home.
* Greet one another face to face and say hello when you walk through the door. Living together is not an excuse for forgetting to pay attention to each other.
* Respect each other's rights for space. Don't hog all the closets

and drawers.

- Learn to live with her favorite painting hanging on the wall. She may be uietly tolerating your golf clubs permanently propped up in the hallway.
- If you get the mail, don't feel free to open your partner's. Living together does not call a halt to privacy.

3. Define your roles.

There are numerous aspects to the roles and relationships of live-in partners. Many who are forging this path have come up with formidable guidelines that foster security and harmony.

• *Determining the status.* The first step is to establish how both the man and woman view themselves within the relationship. Are they more like roommates, a couple, or independent living partners? Each of these roles encompasses a different set of expectations and behaviors. Where there is a perceived difference, there is likely to be problems. To maintain mutual satisfaction, it is mandatory that both participants agree on which category they fit into.

• *Being a couple.* The most serious live-ins frequently perceive themselves as a couple similar to married people. But because the live-in relationship is still viewed as less permanent and less committed than marriage, family, friends, and coworkers are often reticent to take one's live-in partner seriously. On numerous occasions, women interviewed who had lived with men for long periods still reported feeling like mistresses. There were invitations for social functions without their names, business associates failing to address them by name year after year, and their partners' parents not making them feel like family members.

Accepting the role and responsibility of being part of a couple necessitates that both men and women remedy these misperceptions and painful slights. To do otherwise would be harmful to the relationship. These are not unfair expectations to place on one another; no one should expect less of a partner.

• *Voicing your expectations.* Do not assume that your partner knows what you are thinking, feeling, or expecting with respect to your roles. This needs to be voiced. Each individual's perception of appropriate behavior may be different in these circumstances and require defining. This is particularly important when children are involved. Is your live-in supposed to participate in parenting, or is this off limits? Is it important to you that your live-in establish a relationship with your mother and father?

Ask yourself these questions. Discuss them with your partner. Remember, every couple is unique. You need to establish your own roles and guidelines.

4. Maintain your sense of self.

Losing oneself and relinquishing one's identity in a live-in relationship is a problem more often admitted by women interviewed than men. It robs these women of their confidence, strength, and control. Subsequently women who have either been down this road before or who are aware of this potential problem vigilantly guard against it in a number of ways.

"Working makes me feel better about myself," Paula says, "I am responsible for myself. I work a forty- to fifty-hour week and take care of myself. I know I can move out. I know I can support myself."

"The first time I lived with someone, I gave up my friends and limited my activities to be with John," reveals Joanne. "I was totally wrapped up in him. I had no life outside of our relationship. When we broke up after living together for several years, I was at a total loss. I had to start all over again and discover myself and make all new friends. I am living with someone now and have my own life and my own routine."

5. Select a mutually comfortable living arrangement.

Unfortunately, there are no hard and fast rules that make selecting where to live a simple matter. There are dangers in moving into his or her place. While it would seem wise to move into neutral territory where each partner is starting fresh, that isn't always possible.

• *Feeling at home.* Feeling at home, no matter where you choose to live, is a must. You may have to make it happen, especially when you move into his or her house. Insist on paying part of the monthly mortgage or rent if it makes you feel more at home. Claim your space, invite your friends over, and add your touches. One of the women I interviewed asked for all new bed linens to exorcise the ghosts of her lover's previous sleep-ins.

If you have tried everything and still feel like a guest, perhaps you ought to move out. Staying won't do your relationship any good. It is impossible to nurture healthy interaction when two people don't have equal footing within a live-in household.

◆ *Feeling secure*. Feeling secure with any living arrangement is good, plain common sense.

Debbie knew that her relationship with Carl was shaky, but she wanted to live with him anyway. She was careful, however, not to put herself in a precarious position. "I agreed to live with Carl if he would move into my apartment. I wanted to be able to afford living where I was if he moved out." He did, and she could.

◆ *Creative thinking*. Most people are not like Debbie when they decide to move in; they want to take advantage of two salaries and upgrade their living conditions. Here is one suggestion of how to do that and maintain some fairness. Sue earned 60 percent of her and Jim's combined income. The rent was split accordingly. Coming up with your own solution may be your best bet.

6. Get help with your relationship if you need it.

Therapy is not limited to married couples. One therapist reported that at least one-quarter of her patients were unmarried couples.

Stanley wanted Fran to move back in. "No way," she said, "not without seeing a counselor." It turned out to be the same therapist who keeps them on track as Mr. and Mrs.

If you decide to seek professional guidance in your relationship, map out the issues you want to cover and what you want to correct. Establish goals and periodically evaluate whether you are making progress.

DON'TS

1. Don't allow yourself to be talked into live-in love.

Men and women are both guilty of putting on the pressure,

and some will use any ploy to get what they want.

Rodney admits, "I still can't figure out how Maggie got into my home. I was interested in her, but not that interested! I was in my early forties and a guy who had been around. I never thought any woman could pull this on me."

2. Don't move in if you plan to cover up the fact that you are living with your lover.

Hiding your living arrangements from family and friends may add undue pressure to the relationship. When you decide to install separate telephone lines and use a post office box to camouflage your living arrangement, ask yourself why there is need for secrecy. Does it mean that moving in isn't the right or comfortable decision for you? Or does it mean that you aren't proud of your partner and your relationship?

3. Don't slip back into fantasy.

Ann is experienced at live-in love. She is only one of a handful of women I interviewed who decided to give it a third try. This time, however, at thirty-five years of age, she has set up a system of checks and balances to maintain her focus and control.

"You have to check yourself constantly," Ann explains. "If you don't, you could end up terribly hurt six months later. I didn't have the ability or the knowledge ten years ago to ask myself these questions when I lived with Paul.

"When Donald asked me to move in with him, I pulled myself out of the euphoria of being in love and said I would if he planned to marry me and if we could visit my parents and explain all of this to them. We didn't set a definite time frame for our marriage to take place because we both had some financial and personal problems to work out. But in my mind, I set dates for each of us to become fiscally sound, to work out career problems, and to establish better relations with out ex-spouses. Every few months I asked myself: Is where I am right now good for me? Is this relationship better or worse than it was? And can I still bail out if I get stuck?"

4. Don't be more accommodating than is commensurate with his or her commitment.

In her early twenties, Kimberly is trusting, responsible, sweet, compromising, and naive. In his late twenties, Sam is demanding, bossy, and inflexible. Kimberly is looking for a ring and the security of marriage. Sam is avoiding the commitment. When I spoke with Kimberly, she said, "It is really coincidental that you called and wanted to talk to me right now. I am having a problem with Sam. I didn't think he would act like this. I'm not really sure how to handle it.

"I have a job I really like and am making progress in it. I have already been given several raises. Sam is also doing well at his job. Recently, he was asked to open a new office in a city 120 miles away. He didn't ask me if we could move; he *told* me we were moving. I resent that he thinks he can order me around like that. I told him I didn't want to leave, because of my job. He thinks my attitude is silly since he makes more money than I do. I came up with the suggestion that we find a place to live in between the two cities, enabling us to each keep our jobs.

"He gave me two months to come up with an apartment midway. I have been searching but can't find anything that satisfies him. He found a nice place close to his new office and wants to sign the lease. He would have already, but his credit is so bad that without my signature the lease won't be approved."

Sam got the apartment of his choice and did not propose to Kimberly, who is driving 240 miles round-trip to her work daily. The women who have been this route before her would advise Kimberly and others: "Accommodation and concessions should work both ways. Commitment ought to be a two-way street."

5. Don't do anything that makes you feel uncomfortable.

"Todd and I have been living together for a few years. We talk about getting married once all of our individual debts are paid off. I am probably in a bigger hurry than he is and thought we would be man and wife by now. I am thirty-seven and have never been married. I want to have children and feel my biological clock ticking. He is several years older and has been divorced for more than six years.

"I finally paid off my car. For once in my life, I had no car payment to make. It felt great. I was anticipating all the money I could save and how helpful that would be to getting us debt-free and married. But when Todd's car died, he wanted me to give him mine. Together, we picked out a new expensive model for me to drive. This car thing bothers me. I think I am still taking some risks here."

This well-meaning woman would have less to ponder if she stuck to doing what made her feel comfortable.

6. Don't take sex for granted just because you are living together.

Sex is a big part of any relationship. It is a myth that sex automatically goes downhill because two people live together or marry. In fact, the happiest long-term married couples I interviewed for *Marriage Secrets* reported that a sexual relationship can be highly satisfying if you want it to succeed.

You are responsible for the health of your sex lives.

Avoid these falsehoods that surfaced and caused trouble among live-in lovers:

- "My partner should be ready for sex at any time because we live together."
- "It isn't necessary to set the mood for sex once you live together."
- "Sex shouldn't be as important now that we are living together."
- "There isn't a need to experiment with my partner to find better ways to satisfy each other."

7. Don't expect your lover to change when you become live-in lovers, and don't blame yourself when he or she doesn't.

It took twenty-year-old Meagan several years to be able to tell thirty-year-old Jeff, with whom she had fallen madly in love, "No matter what you promise or what you say, you are the same person you were. I can't take it anymore."

What couldn't she take? Jeff was a problem drinker, an uncontrollable gambler, and a womanizer. When Meagan found another woman's telephone number in his pocket, she wanted out.

"She felt like she was doing something wrong," Jeff explains. "She thought she wasn't enough for me to come home to. I knew she was emotionally getting beat-up. There was nothing she could do to change me. I had to change myself. I had to stop being the party boy and grow up. I would have grown up faster if she had not moved in.

"When she decided to leave, I asked her not to go. But she said she would come back only when I was ready to straighten up and get married. She was smart to get out of there. I couldn't have gone straight with her staying with me; it was too easy for me. She could do all the encouraging she wanted to, but I wasn't ready to be good and take on the responsibility of marriage. I put her through a lot of pain. Now that we are married, I try not to think about it. I just try to make her comfortable."

ACHIEVING SUCCESS

Applying the suggestions in this chapter will undoubtedly help many couples to program their relationship for a better try at live-in love. There is no better way to begin the journey to the altar.

CHAPTER 9

Getting to the Altar

No matter what promises are made when two people move in together, there is still work to be done to ensure you get to the altar, if
your ultimate goal is matrimony. Before capturing the titles of Mr.
and Mrs., you will experience tenuous moments that require the art
of gentle persuasion.

A word of caution: As you read about these couples who made
trips to the altar and are currently living happily ever after, don't
block out the memory of those couples who didn't.

SIZING UP THE MARITAL SITUATION

According to Drs. Connell Cowan and Melvyn Kinder, authors of *Women Men Love, Women Men Leave,* young women today
seek a committed relationship but fear that men do not share their
values. Barbara Lovenheim, author of *Beating the Marriage Odds,* offers encouragement to these women. In her survey, 75 percent of
men favored marriage as a lifestyle.

Here are some factors that affect the marital climate in the
1990s:

* Marriage rates are on a downslide because of the numbers
  of couples who choose to cohabit instead of marry.

- Before couples marry today, there is a greater probability that they will live together.
- Couples may enjoy the first year of cohabitation but generally complain of more turbulence the second and third years of living together.
- At least 40 percent of the couples who cohabit break up quickly and do not move on to marriage.
- While 60 percent of men and women who remarried during 1980–1987 cohabited, 14 percent of them married a partner other than the one they lived with.

EXPLORING THE POTENTIAL OF LOVE

Love alone is not enough to create a successful relationship. Still, it is undeniably a potent factor that motivates men and women to take that walk down the aisle.

Therefore, exploring the meaning of love and how to nurture it is a worthwhile endeavor if one's ultimate goal is matrimony.

Defining Love

Researchers agree:

1. The need for love is a fundamental human condition.
2. Love begins with a basic attraction.
3. Romantic, unrealistic love may foster the growth of a deeper love.
4. Love takes time to develop.
5. Love can be nurtured and helped to grow.
6. Mature love encompasses appreciation, concern, passion, and a genuine caring for one's partner.

Nurturing the Growth of Love

Particularly enlightening is a look at love in relation to the "reward–exchange" principle defined by sociologists Letha Dawson Scanzoni and John Scanzoni in *Men, Women, and Change*. Rather than giving love as an end in itself, love is expressed in order to maintain and beget the love of one's partner. The rewards of loving and being loved are exchanged between a couple and perpetuate the love relationship. The growth of love, therefore, is based largely upon the willingness to reciprocate love's rewards.

The rewards to which the Scanzonis refer include:

+ an expression of appreciation and gratitude
+ emotional intimacy through self-disclosure
+ mutual dependency
+ fulfillment of needs
+ enhancement of self-worth.

Consider these practical suggestions to increase your partner's love:

+ Be a good friend and companion.
+ Give support.
+ Tend to your lover's ego.
+ Communicate your love in words and deeds.
+ Express your love openly.
+ Encourage your partner to express love.
+ Show pleasure when your partner acts in a loving manner.
+ Try not to act frustrated with your partner's lack of love.
+ Do not retreat into silence when your partner does.

A Love Test

Now that you know what love is about, ask yourself honestly if it is present in your relationship. If you need help determining whether you or your partner is in love, take the following love test. Begin by asking yourself how you respond to your love interest. Then ask the questions in reference to your lover's behavior.

1. Does my partner tell me he/she loves me?
2. Can I think of two ways my partner shows me he/she loves me?
3. Does my partner care about me and my feelings?
4. Is my partner supportive?
5. Does my partner prefer my company over that of others?

6. Am I my partner's best friend?
7. Does my partner need me?
8. Is my partner attracted to me?
9. Does my partner act passionately toward me?
10. Does my partner think I am wonderful?

A total of ten "yeses" is a good score.

LOVE STORIES

Romantic love—that irresistible, compelling attraction that escapes definition—can defy reason and still emerge victorious. When it does, however, it more often applies to those rare, real-life fairy tales that elude the majority of lovers.

Still in the romantic stages, although not blinded by love when they moved in together, the next two couples had a vision of the enduring love they would find with one another. It was the promise of this love that prompted them to become live-in lovers, a route that eventually led to the commitment of marriage.

The Rush of Love

When I spoke with Lenny, twenty-five, and Leslie, twenty-one, their wedding date was six months away. They had moved in together only months after they met and became engaged a year and a half later.

"I know it sounds kooky," admits Lenny, "but I think it was true love. It just hit us. I was immediately attracted to Leslie. We met on the job in New York, where I was living temporarily after my Reserve unit had served in the Gulf War. Leslie was modeling, and I was doing the photography. Things moved quickly. You really get to know somebody when you work with them eighteen hours a day.

"I was moving to San Francisco," Lenny says, "and wanted to visit my parents that weekend before I left. I invited Leslie to come along. It was supposed to be just a friendly trip, but after that weekend I knew I loved her.

"Once I was out on the West Coast, she came to see me for two weeks. I ended up coming back with her. I wasn't planning to stay, but I ended up moving in with her. We were both ready to quit the bar and club scene and had a good idea of what we wanted out of life. I was definitely committed when I moved in," Lenny explains. "I wasn't ambivalent at all whether I should or shouldn't. We both knew it was a crazy thing to do so quickly, but we were glad we did it. The basis of our live-in relationship was definitely love. Everything else, like friendship and convenience, was secondary. Leslie is a very wise woman, and even though she was so young, she had a deep understanding of what creates a good relationship."

Leslie interjects, "I knew after four months that he was the man I wanted to spend my life with. I graduated from high school early and went to college when I was sixteen. I went wild and dated tons of guys. When Lenny and I met, I was in a pretty good relationship with someone else. But when I got to know Lenny, I discovered how two people should feel about one another. There was love and a sense of security that I had never had with anyone else.

"I didn't think about what we were doing when Lenny moved in," Leslie admits. "I just knew he was serious and that it was right because I loved him. It wasn't a trial period. It wasn't like we'll see how this goes. We had already determined we wanted to spend our lives together; I wouldn't have let him move in otherwise. I had never lived with anyone. It wasn't strained at all having him move in, but my best friend, who shared the apartment with me, was extremely apprehensive. We all lived together for a year.

"From the beginning," Leslie continues, "we told each other we would be completely honest. We didn't want to screw each other up. If we had a problem, we discussed it. No head games. That way we developed the best friendship, too."

Lenny says, "We both knew we were meant for each other and set our wedding date after a year and a half living together. We could go on living together, but we love each other so much that we want to tie ourselves together even more. So why mess around? Marriage is an expression of our commitment. It is on a higher plane. So many people tell us that we should have taken more time before we moved in and now before we marry, but Leslie and I agree that it doesn't make any difference. There isn't anything we would do differently."

Love at Last

Chuck had a live-in relationship for four years before he met Samantha. He was never in love during the four-year relationship, and it ended painfully. He said, "Never again," to living together. But when he fell in love with Samantha, all of that changed.

"Chuck fell in love first," says Samantha, a pretty and vivacious woman in her late twenties. "His friends told me he was completely in love with me."

It didn't take Samantha long to return Chuck's love. "Chuck was different from the other guys I had dated," she says. "He was older and more mature. I was flattered by the way he treated me. He put me first and was so thoughtful and respectful. He really is a wonderful, exceptional man. I got lucky. I loved him by the time he asked me to move in a few months later.

"It happened quickly. We were living one hundred miles apart when we met, but I was in the middle of moving back home, where Chuck was living. Rather than move in with my mom, I moved in with Chuck. You don't rush into this sort of thing unless you have a Chuck in your life. I knew I could move home if it didn't work out. I really thought there was a good chance for this relationship to lead to marriage. He was definitely the kind who wanted to marry, even though he had been a bachelor for so long. I wanted to move in to see if I could live with him, because in the past I would go away for a weekend with a guy and find that I couldn't stand him. I was surprised when Chuck asked me to marry him three weeks after I moved in," Samantha reveals.

"We are talking about a very good relationship since the beginning," Chuck says, explaining his speedy proposal. "As soon as she moved in, I backed off some of my other activities. I wanted to be with her. I was in love and more sincere than the first time I lived with a woman. I felt like I got to know Samantha quickly. There was an instant comfort zone. I guess it could have gone wrong because I proposed while I was still completely infatuated by her. But my first instinct was that she was the right one."

"We were both products of broken homes," Samantha says, "and we both took marriage seriously. If and when either of us did marry, we intended it to be a forever thing."

Five years later, Samantha and Chuck are on the road to lasting love with two babies inhabiting their happy household.

LIVING TOGETHER, A PREREQUISITE FOR MARRIAGE

Liza and Tim are one of several couples interviewed for whom living together was a prerequisite to matrimony. The experience offered them the forum to address practical considerations. This attitude was most often voiced by men or women who had experienced divorce.

Liza, married and in her mid-thirties, fell in love with Tim, married and in his late thirties. Before they took the giant step forward and married, they lived together to test the endurance of their love.

"It is hard to talk about how Tim and I got together," Liza begins. "Of all the things either of us has done in our lives, this is one that both of us feel the most guilty about. It was so completely out of character for either of us not to be faithful to our spouses. We worked together for a long time before the chemical and emotional attraction between us became so intense that we could not ignore it any longer. We finally admitted our mutual attraction at an office Christmas party, but we did not begin an intimate relationship right away. I went to work somewhere else and Tim would come and take me to lunch or wait for me after work just to grab a little time together.

"Tim left his wife four weeks after the party. We were both out of control. It wasn't just a physical thing. There was a real bond between us, something spiritual. I look upon our love as a blessing," Liza explains. "Once I fell in love with Tim, I realized that I was not in love with my husband. I was honest with him about what was happening. We went to a marriage counselor, and she told my husband that he ought to allow me to see Tim to determine if the relationship was what I thought it was. She told him that I would anyway, and maybe I would get him out of my system. Otherwise, she said, there wouldn't be any hope for us.

"Tim was pressing me. He couldn't understand why I still lived in my house after he had already left his wife. But I had been married for seven years and had two children, ages one and three. After four months, I did leave, and my husband was totally devastated. Alcohol had already played a big part in his life, and now it turned him into a basket case. He couldn't even work. Tim wanted to take care of me and the children. He felt responsible. He helped pay for a very nice apartment in a secure building, where I lived with the children for eight months, safely protected from my husband's fury."

At the same time that Liza's lease came up for renewal, Tim purchased a house that would accommodate a family, and Liza helped select it and decorate. When Tim moved in, so did Liza and her children.

"I knew that I wanted to marry Tim, and I had no doubt that we would at some point. Tim was having difficulty thinking about getting married right away and needed more time. He wanted to make sure that if he remarried, it was absolutely to the right individual. He also wanted to make sure that we could work as a family unit and that he could be a father. He said that he wouldn't be able to live in a house and not be a participating parent."

Variations of Tim's concerns were expressed by a number of men and women interviewed. A young man with custody of his son said he only married his second wife after he saw how she interacted with his child on a daily basis. Another man in his mid-twenties who had never been married fell in love with a woman several years older with three young children. He moved in to see if he could live happily with them.

Liza acknowledges in retrospect, "It was emotionally dangerous turning myself and the kids over to Tim. But I knew that he was a man of great integrity who took his responsibilities seriously. I also didn't want to take the chance of losing what we had. It was too valuable. I knew that our relationship was more important to him than almost anything—his career or where he lived. He always put my kids first and even signed them up for a prepaid college program. I also knew I would be strong enough to get out of my marriage. I knew I could take care of myself and move home to a carriage house behind my parents' home.

"By the time I moved in, I wasn't walking around blindly in love anymore," Liza says. "Even though Tim said there were no guarantees that we would get married, I thought that living together would get the wheels in motion. It was hard for me to live with him with a couple of children. I wasn't brought up that way, and my parents couldn't understand why we didn't get married after all we had gone through. It was very hard for me to accept the wrath of my family. His parents, on the other hand, were very much a part of our lives from the beginning. They could see how much in love he was and accepted me and my children because I made him so happy.

"Looking back—despite the problem with my family—I think living together was valuable for both of us," Liza admits. "I probably wouldn't have married Tim without living with him first. We both had to stop doubting that marriage could work. I did not want to live together as long as we did before we got married. Six months would have been plenty, but Tim needed more time to adjust. While I resented him for it at the time, I knew it would be foolish to leave. I knew he was a fair person, and I trusted him completely.

"We did a lot of talking during the year we lived together, which helped him prepare for marriage. He was feeling a tremendous guilt about what he did to his wife and to me. I was trying to make him work through all of that. I was forcing him to express himself. I kept telling him it wouldn't work unless we talked about what was bothering us. Whenever he was in a bad mood or full of anger, I made him sit in a hot tub and talk. I was insistent about that.

"I had to be careful, because I'm the type who easily compromises. But I wasn't going to allow him to take total charge. I let him know what I expected when it came to the children and to living as a family. For one, I was not as strict as he is and absolutely did not believe in spanking. I would never tolerate that kind of discipline. Secondly, there was no way I would tolerate his habit of going out after work for a few drinks with his colleagues before coming home.

"When we learned we could live within each other's guidelines,

Tim started talking marriage and decided he wanted to have his own children. I became pregnant before we even had time to set our wedding date. A few weeks later we were married in front of a group of our closest friends."

STRATEGIC POINTERS

Progressing from a live-in relationship to matrimony generally requires more than the momentum of love. The couples in this section advocate:

* making your goals understood
* standing your ground
* proceeding with confidence
* maintaining your conviction
* paying attention to your partner's responses
* looking for pivotal moments and being ready to act.

It is also noteworthy to point out that the men in the following two lessons valued marriage and looked forward to being part of a family before they met their brides. Just as important are the strength, self-control, and insight these women exhibited at critical moments.

Lesson 1: Lou, Setting His Sights on Matrimony

Lou's divorce after six years of marriage was traumatic for him. "I wasn't interested in divorce. I was deeply disappointed when my marriage failed. I had never really planned to be single again," he says. By the time he met Julia, twenty-four, he was thirty-three, had been separated for two years, and had made a good adjustment living alone. "I was feeling pretty happy about my transition, but my goal was definitely to remarry. When I dated I looked at each woman as a potential mate."

However, when he picked out Julia, she was thinking along different lines despite her immediate attraction to Lou.

"It was that cornball thing," says Julia, describing how she felt about Lou when they started dating. "Like when you know within weeks that he's the right one for you." But Julia wasn't thinking "right" in terms of marriage. In fact, she had been telling her family and friends for years that she never planned to marry or have children. "I wanted to have a very long relationship with Lou, but I didn't want to think about marriage. My parents had divorced and, being the eldest of six children, I helped raise my brothers and sisters.

"It was my idea to move in with Lou," Julia admits. "We had been dating a year and a half when I told him I wanted to give my apartment to my brother and move in with Lou. I was really angry when Lou wasn't too keen on the idea," Julia explains.

"I wasn't really interested in living with anyone at the time," Lou admits. "I was eager to find a permanent mate and begin a family. I didn't want to waste time living with someone. At first I said no. But living together was appealing because we would have more time together and a more convenient and private sexual relationship. Most of all, I thought there was a good chance that the relationship would become permanent and was worth the emotional risk I was taking."

Being a lawyer, Lou was adept at presenting his case for marriage. When the subject periodically came up with Julia, Lou would always remark, "Why do I meet these independent women who don't want to get married when that is what I want?" Then he would argue, "Marriage is just a document that makes a partnership legal. If you have a great partnership, why wouldn't you want to make it legal and announce it to the world?"

Julia's typical response to his case: "I thought that was very romantic, but I wasn't ready to change my mind—at least in the beginning."

As time went on, however, Julia began to take Lou's argument a little more seriously.

"I know I made it clear to Julia that I wanted to be married," Lou stresses. "But I was also calculating the feedback I was getting from Julia, which was negative. So I toned down the tempo a little and decided to be patient. I was hearing some *positive* things from her, too, which gave me reason to believe her viewpoint was changing. She was interested in moving out of New York to a city upstate that was much more conducive to the type of family lifestyle I was interested in. I took that as a good sign."

Lou and Julia had lived together a year by the time they moved out of the city and Lou became more insistent on marriage. "I was in my mid-thirties and heard a clock ticking," he says. "I felt like I was getting behind in starting my family and reaching my goal. There wasn't any one specific conversation or incident that brought the issue to a head, so I can't say I gave Julia an ultimatum. But I do remember communicating in various ways that I did not want to waste my time. If she didn't agree to marry me, I would have broken off the relationship and started a new search for a permanent mate." Julia got the message.

"I can't pinpoint exactly why I finally agreed to get engaged. My attitude started to change slowly when we moved out of the city. Within six months, I realized that I loved Lou so much that I did not want to deny him something he wanted so much, and on top of that I was running out of reasons why we shouldn't get married. One of my reasons had been, 'What's wrong with the way we are now?' That didn't make sense anymore. I didn't want to lose him. It would have been too hurtful for me to end the relationship, and I knew he wouldn't agree to continue our relationship unless I made plans to get married. I also found out that I had a lot of maternal instincts and wanted to have children. I think it all changes when you love someone."

Married for seven years and with several children, Julia and Lou still have differing opinions on marriage and living together. "I haven't found anything significantly different about being married," Julia points out.

Lou, on the other hand, argues, "I think that there is a big difference. Marriage is more stable. You need that formal commitment for an unequivocal understanding that both parties are committed to a relationship."

The rhetoric is no longer of any consequence. Julia and Lou are both happy. And Lou got what he wanted—a trip to the altar.

◆　◆　◆

Lesson 2: Shana, Pushing to Her Limit

At twenty-one, Shana was rather astute about the nature of men and relationships when she met thirty-one-year-old Paul, who was just recovering from the pain of a broken love affair. "My goal was to marry Paul. He was someone I wanted to share my life with, and that was the bottom line," admits Shana, now his wife of eight years. "I knew that he was just coming out of a serious and very passionate relationship and that it would be best for us to become friends before we became lovers. Subconsciously, I made myself indispensable to Paul. You know how your best friend is indispensable and you can't imagine life without that person for all the emotional support and understanding he or she gives you. I made it so he wouldn't want to lose me."

Shana's plan was effective. Paul fell in love with her, and when he took a job out of town he asked Shana to go with him and move in. "I was nervous moving in with Shana after my other live-in relationship, but in a way I felt more comfortable this time," Paul says. "We were both much more open about what we needed. I knew if I had a problem I could go to her. She was my best friend and stronger and more mature than the other woman I had had relationships with. Shana helped me out a lot and was her own person, not an appendage I had to take care of. I think we were both very serious and committed to the relationship when we moved."

"I can't say it all happened just the way I wanted it to," Shana says with a little regret. "I am kind of traditional and like the idea of a big wedding, which doesn't seem appropriate after living with someone for three years. I'm really not all for living together, but moving with Paul was important, and there was no way I could afford to go with him unless we lived together. I wasn't naive enough to think that marriage would automatically follow living together, but I did know that Paul was a really wonderful man and that there weren't a lot like him around.

"I worked hard at the relationship to show Paul that we could do well together. At the same time, I really kept tabs on what was happening and where the relationship was going. I was not going to let the whole thing run away with me. I think basically we shared the same values and both wanted a traditional life with children. We both firmly believed in marriage. All of that and Paul's goodness made me feel I was doing the right thing.

"I think everything would have gone smoothly except Paul had a serious career setback and was out of work for four months, making him feel desperate. This totally deflated his ego. I was supporting both of us entirely. He got real down in the mouth and felt very insecure. He didn't have a lot of self-worth after having the door shut on him over and over again.

"One day he just told me he was going home in such a way that it sounded like, 'Come if you want; if not, goodbye.' I was furious and hurt," Shana remembers. "I said, 'After all I've been though with you, you are going to pick up and leave me here?' I thought we were thinking along the same lines, but obviously at this point we weren't. I panicked. I thought his commitment wasn't anything near mine. I was really scared. I wasn't sure whether to stay or go or what. I suppose I could have walked out the door," Shana says, "but that wasn't an option. I loved him.

"Instead, I encouraged him to stay a little longer and give himself more time. And I made it clear that if he decided to move back, there was no way I would have gone with him without a firm commitment. I had my limits!

"He got a good job offer the next week," Shana notes, "and boom—he turned back into the person I trusted and felt secure with. But I remember saying to him that we would have to start talking about why he might have left and figure out if it was all the job or really part of the relationship. I wanted to know where I stood."

For several months following this crisis, the subject of marriage would periodically come up while Paul and Shana sat at their kitchen table. Shana grew impatient with Paul's wavering and finally called his bluff. Handing him a calendar that hung on their wall, she told him, "Okay, if we are getting married, pick a date."

"I took the bull by the horns, and within fifteen minutes we had picked a date," Shana recalls. "Now we laugh at other people's romantic engagements."

"I didn't take Shana's statement as an ultimatum," Paul explains. "I felt she was just being honest about her feelings. If you aren't comfortable enough with the person you want to spend your life with to express yourself out in the open, then something is wrong. It wasn't that I didn't want to marry her; I needed an extra push."

MAKING DISTINCTIONS BETWEEN LIVING TOGETHER AND BEING MARRIED

There should no longer be room for doubt that moving in, with or without the benefit of ample amounts of love, is not sufficient cause to book the caterer and select a wedding gown.

However, if you are willing to accept that living together is not like being married, you will have an advantage when lobbying for matrimony. Holding some incentives and rewards in reserve for when you become Mr. and Mrs. may entice your reluctant partner to take that long walk down the aisle.

Perfect Junctures

There are optimal moments for the strategist to make a move in the direction of marriage from a live-in relationship. The most obvious arise when buying a house, deciding to have children, or making a move out of town or to another apartment. If your partner is willing to make this type of overt commitment, why not the more subtle, loving one of marriage?

Be on the lookout for less conspicuous moments that provide perfect junctures in your relationship to press the issue and point out the rewards of being marriage partners instead of live-in lovers. This may include such simple situations as being requested to accompany your partner and his or her parents on a family vacation. There is nothing wrong with replying, "But I am not a member of your family yet," or "I can't take you on this business trip; it is for husbands and wives."

Get your argument down pat before you approach a lover who is dragging his or her feet. No doubt any argument will meet with a rebuttal on the first attempt. Be sure how far you intend to go before beginning this discussion and then stand tall and firm making your point.

Providing Inviting Images

To provide images that will invite your partner to take a step toward matrimony, you must first begin by setting up some clear cut distinctions in your own mind. For instance:

- How much are you willing to give, compromise, or sacrifice within a live-in relationship?
- How far are you willing to look into the future and commit to plans with a lover that is not a marriage partner?
- How would your commitment toward your lover differ between a marriage and a live-in relationship?

Once you have searched within yourself for the picture that marriage holds for you and have a firm handle on what you see as the differences between matrimony and living together, you will be equipped to paint a vivid and deliciously appealing image to your lover of what awaits him or her. If you firmly believe in the pleasures and rewards that marriage offers, you can clearly present these points to your live-in partner.

The promise of something better—a more intense, loving, caring, and enduring relationship—is a start. How about the image of a more available, compromising, and understanding mate—one who is guaranteed to be on call during the inevitable strains and stresses of life we all experience? Use some of the arguments presented in this book by lovers who have found marriage preferable.

Among the pluses people in my book *Marriage Secrets* revealed are:

- a sense of peace, contentment, purpose, and completeness
- genuine happiness and fulfillment
- a lifetime cheerleader and best friend
- a partner in life's journey
- a confidence and ego booster
- love, respect, and fulfillment of needs
- a sharing of goals of dreams.

◆ ◆ ◆

Getting to the altar is merely the first step in replacing live-in love with matrimony. The second step is acting wisely to improve the marriage forecast.

CHAPTER 10

Improving the Marriage Forecast

Just because your wedding date is set does not mean that you are out of the trap zone of live-in love. Beware! According to the research of Jay D. Teachman, Jeffrey Thomas, and Kathleen Paasch of the University of Maryland, the partnerships formed between legally married individuals are more stable than those of men and women who live together without a legal union. Furthermore, after marriage the unions of those who lived together prior to marriage remain less stable than couples who began living together with the legal sanctions of matrimony.

Chapter 6 shed partial light on these findings. This chapter completes the picture and identifies prudent behavior and wise attitudes that increase the chances for martial stability after living together.

THE MATTER OF COMPATIBILITY

According to much current research, it is a reasonable but false assumption that living together filters out incompatible partners more effectively than traditional dating. The large numbers of men and women who cohabit and divorce bear this out. If couples are going to use living together to determine their compatibility, it is imperative that they use an improved standard of measurement.

Setting up a Compatibility Test

Here are two variations of the compatibility test. Both Lou's and Kathy's experiences are instructive for setting up your own test. It is not accidental that Lou and Kathy were both married and divorced before determining the need to devise these tests. Live-in lovers who have been through divorce tend to be cautious when considering remarriage. The compatibility tests that these couples have devised will benefit anyone in a live-in relationship, regardless of whether they previously experienced a marital partnership.

Lou's Test

1. Begin with the right attitude. Lou, the attorney you met in Lesson 1 in the last chapter, was looking for a marriage partner when he met Julia. He has some good ideas on compatibility testing. "If people are going to live together," he explains, "they ought to take advantage of the opportunity and really learn about each other. Don't squander living together by being content with convenient sex and sharing household responsibilities. Otherwise you won't get the full benefit out of it."

2. Know what you are looking for in a marriage partner. Lou wanted a lover, a friend, a wife, and a good mother for the children he hoped to have some day.

3. Make a checklist of the most important qualities you expect in a partner and see how your intended stacks up. Lou did this and is not embarrassed to admit, "I don't want it to sound coldly calculating, because part of the checklist is what you are feeling and not just thinking, but if you are looking to get married and using living together to determine your compatibility, you have to be partly emotional and partly rational. If you aren't examining both aspects, you are taking a big risk."

4. Try to be clear sighted. The first time Lou lived with a woman, he wasn't. Living together led to marriage and divorce. He wasn't about to make the same mistake twice. Lou knew he loved

Julia, but how did he know she could be more of what he needed to give marriage a brighter outlook?

"I had a conversation with myself," Lou explains methodically. "I was focused. I knew I could still make a mistake in judgment, but at least I tried to make a better determination. I looked at the way Julia related to her family and me. I saw how good she made others around her feel. When we lived together I became convinced that she was quite capable of being a nurturing mate and mother."

5. *Measure how well you are able to relate to one another.* Lou based his assessment on concrete issues. "We were compatible sexually and intellectually," he recalls. "I enjoyed talking with Julia. I knew that despite some of her early hesitations we wanted the same things out of our relationship."

6. *Determine the potential to be accommodating.* If you or your partner is stubborn and won't budge to end a stalemate or restore peace and harmony to your relationship, that is the first sign you may be incompatible. Lou notes that in his case living together gave him and Julia the opportunity to see how their two personalities meshed under the same roof. "We were both insightful and perceptive during the process, carefully evaluating each other's responses," Lou emphasizes. "We took this time to see if we could adjust to each other's idiosyncrasies, strengths, and weaknesses. How you deal with them, I think, determines how happy or unhappy you will be as a marriage."

Lou's test proved very effective. "Our marriage is very satisfying. I think I had realistic expectations after living with Julia, and our marriage is meeting those. I don't think I could be happier," he concludes with well-earned satisfaction.

Kathy's Two-Step Test

Kathy's motivation to move in with Tom did not initially focus on a compatibility test. When Kathy, at age thirty-six, met Tom and fell in love after a year and half of dating, she had been divorced for five years and was ready to remarry. Tom looked like a good candidate. Kathy thought that moving in would not only lead toward matrimony but also afford her the opportunity to make some changes in Tom's behavior. Quickly enough, however, she realized that what she objected to were deeply embedded and not easily altered personality traits. That's when she decided that a compatibility test was in order.

Kathy needed to determine whether she would, in fact, be able to live with Tom for better or for worse. Here is how she did it:

1. Kathy took off her rose-colored glasses. "Living with Tom burst my bubble and made me see I would have to be more realistic. We were not able to sustain the passion, the hearts and flowers romantic part of our relationship, that was there in the beginning. Instead, living with him at times was so difficult that had we not gone through this before getting married, I would have been devastated and our marriage would probably have failed.

"Sharing a home did not increase my influence over Tom the way I thought it would," Kathy continues with the candor that has colored her vision for much of the last dozen years. "I could not change the fact that Tom was very headstrong and would accept things only one way—his. He was not willing to alter his eating habits, his nights out with the boys, or his evenings on the couch. There was absolutely no way to engage him in a discussion about our relationship or his behavior. I came to the conclusion that he was incapable of the kind of love I admired between my parents. Tom was different than my father, who preferred my mother's company over everyone else's. Tom is a man's man.

"He was very honest about himself," Kathy reveals, "and told me that he knew he would not be an easy person to live with. In fact, once when we were dating I remarked that I wanted to spend the rest of my life with him and he replied, 'No, you don't. I am not a good guy to be married to.'

"It is true that if I were writing a love story," Kathy admits, "It wouldn't be written this way."

2. Kathy calculated what she would get out of a marriage relationship with Tom and determined whether it would be enough to satisfy her. The picture, even without rose-colored glasses, isn't all that bleak, Kathy reassures me. "I was looking for companionship, love, and financial security. I would be lying if I didn't say that was important. I had struggled going to school and getting a job. Working was fine, but my income looked better when it became my secondary, not primary, source of revenue. There were definitely pros and cons about marring Tom, but I looked at the total package. Some of the things that were missing weren't that significant to me. I was really into maintaining my own independence, so the fact that he wanted to spend a lot of time on his own was not a problem.

"When Tom said to me one day, 'We'll get married in a month,' I was prepared to say yes. I had come to terms with myself about the kind of marriage I was getting into. There was absolutely no doubt that things would have to be done his way. I would fit into a certain slot between his work, his friends, his children, and his activities. He made me promise that I could live with all that," Kathy says, continuing her honest exposé of her live-in relationship and marriage.

"The only thing I made Tom promise was that he would be faithful. Infidelity was the one thing I could not tolerate. We agreed on financial arrangements and negotiated a solid picture of a future for both of us."

Was Kathy's compatibility test accurate? She offers as proof of her successful testing: "I have a level of contentment and happiness that exists within this relationship. I appreciate our home and that we have each other. All of these things are warm and meaningful to me after twelve years. Tom is even starting to mellow a little, but I have no illusions that he is about to change. I got just about what I bargained for and agreed I could live with."

Unexpected Compatibility Testers

Most people think that passing their own compatibility test, whether carefully planned as Lou's and Kathy's or more serendipitous as most, ensures them marital success. That is only part of this rigorous exam. Passing the unexpected compatibility tests that challenge the strength of your relationship and your ability to handle adversity together is the other significant portion.

In fact, there are a noticeable number of married couples who attribute much of their current marital satisfaction to having successfully overcome hurdles that arose while living together. Working through cumbersome problems together created a stronger bond between these men and women and fortified their relationship with the conviction that they could survive any and all future trials and tribulations.

Most of the unexpected twists that challenged the younger, less experienced couples interviewed related to money matters and career upheavals. A few young couples dealt with more serious complications such as unplanned pregnancies or even drug abuse. Teddy and Olivia's compatibility test bombarded them with numerous tricky situations during their live-in relationship. They survived and have a happy seven-year marriage to boast about.

Facing a Mountain of Adversity

Teddy and Olivia became good friends and helpmates before they became lovers. Teddy was new in the United States, a successful European tennis pro who in his mid-twenties moved here to make a bigger name for himself. When he met Olivia, unhappily married and neglected by her rich husband, who happened to be Teddy's American sponsor, becoming involved with her was far from his mind. "The last thing that I thought about was falling in love with a married woman five years older than myself who had two children, let alone marrying her," admits Teddy for openers. "But being with Olivia was very comfortable. She became someone I could really talk to, someone who gave me support and encouragement."

The benefits of this friendship were mutual. "I was left alone a lot with the kids," begins Olivia, a pretty, soft-spoken woman. "Teddy would stay with us now and then. He would come in, and we would sit and talk. He was a confidant who offered me great comfort. Nothing happened even though there was a strong attraction between us until I left my husband. Teddy was careful to protect his reputation and did not want to tarnish his good name by becoming party to an extramarital affair."

Olivia and Teddy approached their relationship carefully, but the swift pace with which it developed may have overwhelmed Teddy a tad. He had after all made the move across the sea to concentrate on his career, not a woman or marriage. The whole affair went against his genuine moral fervor. Despite the real love they felt for each other, Olivia and Teddy encountered problems the year they lived together, threatening the survival of their relationship. For one, Olivia's husband made several unpleasant threats about the custody of their children and made life-threatening ones to Teddy. At one point, Teddy had to hide out for a few days to escape his dangerous fury.

Second, Teddy admits, "My career was going nowhere. I had gone from being somebody who was well respected and feeling good about himself to someone who had no money and a lover whose ex-husband was giving me a bad time. Olivia in a way was even supporting me when I moved into her house. She bought the groceries and would not let me pay her any rent even though things were tight for both of us. I was making no contributions to her except the love and support that I gave her. I suffered a real loss of self-respect and at times felt like going back to Europe. Most of the time I kept this to myself, although Olivia probably knew what I was thinking. I know she understood the pressure I felt going into this relationship with so many things against us.

"It wasn't just the insecurity and uncertainty of my career that made this difficult for me, but there were Olivia's two children to deal with as well, three and five at the time," Teddy reveals. "I had never lived with anyone's children, and they became the cause of most of our arguments. I came from a very disciplined home where my father's word was the law. There was no discussion, that was it. Olivia and I didn't agree at all how to handle these children. I was angry when I saw how hard she tried to please them, doing everything for them but getting no respect in return. Because I was only twenty-six, it was also hard to accept that the children were Olivia's first priority and everything had to be scheduled around them. It was tough, but I knew that Olivia and her kids came as a package.

"It had been a hard year, but we were still crazy about each other. Getting through all of our problems, especially with her husband, made us as close as two people could possibly be," Teddy announces. "Our relationship was definitely formulated on our friendship and mutual understanding. That isn't to say we didn't have a great sex life, too, but Olivia is strong and intelligent and was a pillar of strength to me. When she brought up the subject of marriage at the end of our year together, I was in a better position. I was finally happy, and things were beginning to happen with my career. I had given up the idea of playing professionally and found a really good position managing a first-class tennis complex."

"By the time we married," Olivia notes, confirming the troubled times Teddy related, "we knew we could handle anything that might come along."

Long-term Compatibility

Ted and Olivia's experiences coupled with a multitude of other cases reveal what is at the very core of long-term compatibility:

1. The ability to please and appease one another.
2. The desire to be flexible for the good of the relationship.
3. The dedication to respect, support, and unselfishly love each other.
4. The willingness to make sacrifices for one another.
5. The commitment to work at making the love relationship flourish.

Without these essential attitudes, there is no way to ensure marital satisfaction in the best of times, let alone during the inevitable ups and downs that are part of every lifelong marital experience.

SETTING BETTER PRECEDENTS

It is time to concentrate on the fruitful conduct used by experienced live-in lovers to create a better marriage forecast. Don't shy away from their tactics or delay in getting started. Wisely use fruitful conduct to avoid the hazardous and critical early years of marriage. Divorce rates soar between the second and fifth year of marriage, so be smart: Secure your future happiness before the wedding bells ring.

◆　◆　◆

Fruitful Conduct

In addition to heeding all of the do's and don'ts explored in Chapter 8 and steering clear of the poor precedents exposed in Chapter 5, begin using the following tips:

1. By all means, communicate.

Happily married couples who were live-in lovers revealed that communicating was the key to their good start in matrimony. There is no replacement for the honest, open exchange these couples relied upon to explore ambivalent feelings, disappointments, and complaints before they took their vows. However, be sure to balance these conversations with positive notes by sounding the trumpets for the love and pleasures you gain from your relationship. And by all means, learn how to communicate in a constructive manner—no hitting below the belt, no nasty comments you wished you could retrieve later. Experiment until you discover the most positive and effective way to express your message or draw your partner out to express his.

2. Assume some of the demeanor befitting a good spouse.

First this strategy is more appropriate and less risky for those live-ins who are engaged and have a wedding cake. It is probably too demanding a strategy for anyone in a less committed live-in relationship to bother adopting.

Second, it is mandatory that one accept the fact that a good marital relationship is predicated upon a genuine partnership that develops over time. It is this budding partnership that we witnessed among the best of live-in lovers who went on to happy matrimony. Comfortably they presented themselves as a couple to family and friends and treated each other with the respect due marital partners paving their way toward an enduring family unit. The concessions, compromises, and considerations that good partnerships are made of were evident in the early live-in patterns they set. They made each other a priority and attempted to fulfill each other's reasonable needs and desires.

You can't expect to develop a relationship it takes years of marriage to nurture in a short time, but you can begin working on it as soon as a lifetime commitment is made. Set the precedent for an enviable marital partnership as soon as possible.

In more concrete terms, make your house a home and your live-in partner the most important person in your life. Help him or her fulfill family obligations and begin the arduous work of developing the skills and friendship needed for long-term compatibility.

3. Make your expectations clear.

Determine what you expect from married life and present this to your partner. Be up-front and open. This lessens the chance for any misunderstanding, disappointment, and resentment. Talk about the kind of behavior, interaction, and activities that will help build your marital relationship, and discuss the limits of your tolerance for behavior that won't. Define your attitudes on lifestyle, children, and career plans. Explain how you fit into each other's lives. If you aren't ready for this kind of talk, you are most likely not ready for marriage.

4. Recognize the need for space.

Living together requires a serious evaluation of one's space and often becomes an issue when two people first move in with one another. The novelty propels some men and women to assume an exaggerated and unhealthy mode of togetherness. "Sue wanted all of my attention when we moved into the same apartment," Charles confides. Let's hope Sue wised up like Kitty. Her live-in lover and now husband of four years explains, "Kitty always gave me ample room to do the best job I could, even though I know she wished we had more time together. My career was demanding, and she understood that. She still does."

5. Clear the air of potentially troubling issues.

Before marring their respective partners, Bryant cleared up his drinking problem and Susie rid herself of the harmful emotions collected from her father's neglect of her as a young child. Without taking these prudent actions, their marriage forecasts would have been bleak. Everyone's issues are different, but the need to resolve them, large and small, before marriage is paramount.

Sally says, "We hardly argued at all the first year we were married. We did all of that the year we lived together." She and her young husband were smart to clear the air. What was their most problematic issue? Money, the major source of contention in many married households. You may as well get out the ledger and devise your fiscal policy during those live-in days. Get your rounds over with before the marital event begins.

Sex is another primary issue. Kevin and Kimberly had ailing sexual appetites for two young live-ins planning to marry. When sex became as infrequent as once a month, arguments ensued. Kevin and Kimberly realized that part of their inactivity was due to excessive overweight on both sides, and they began reducing in the hopes of awakening their slumbering libidos before their wedding date. At our last meeting, they were a new and more slender Mr. and Mrs. Kevin Jones who radiated happiness and enthusiasm about their marriage.

THE QUESTION IS: WHEN TO MARRY?

Some women felt that the time they lived with their partners prior to marriage was too long. Just as common were the men who said, "I would have preferred to wait another year or two before we got married. Living together a little longer would have suited me fine." Here is something to get you both thinking about each other's marital readiness and the implications it has on your future: Research reveals that couples who live together for a shorter period of time are less likely to face marital dissolution than couples who cohabit long-term. It is wise, therefore, to ask yourself and your partner some pertinent questions lest you allow live-in love to linger dangerously.

1. Is my partner getting annoyed or angry by putting off a wedding date?

2. Is delaying our marriage hurting or helping our relationship?

3. What would be gained or lost by waiting to marry?

4. Are the excuses my partner gives me about waiting to marry valid?

5. Is it time to compromise and pick a date that satisfies us both?

Timing is of the utmost importance, so don't fail to give it the consideration it deserves.

MAKING A FRESH START

Armed with important information, better precedents, the resolve to succeed, you have just about completed your course for a better marriage forecast. To cap off the lesson, begin anew by making a fresh start in matrimony:

1. Get ready to create a new era of love and excitement.
It isn't very hard to muster these emotions or a hardy enthusiasm for taking your turn at the altar. Recently I spoke with several women who had been part of long-term live-in relationships and who were married or had recently planned their weddings. They sounded like the giddy inexperienced brides of days past. Working on the wedding plans with their grooms added to the anticipation of arriving at a new and exciting plateau in their lives. And for you men whose female live-ins would have preferred matrimony awhile back or who feel that their wedding day may lack the romance of less involved couples, why not shower her with flowers and love notes? Renew the fervor that brought you together in the beginning and intensify it with new expressions of your affection and commitment. Show sincere and mutual delight in knowing that you are determined to enjoy each other for a lifetime.

2. Pack away any of the indecision or difficulties of your live-in days.
Use the period of recreated romantic euphoria to bury any and all scars from the stresses and strains of live-in love and break down the walls that previously separated you. Harriet admits, "Once we were married, it was like a barrier was taken down. I was willing to go and do things that I absolutely refused to before we married, like looking for a home. I knew that we had that ultimate commitment,

and I could really trust James and myself not to go walking out the door. It was a new mental attitude more than anything. I was willing to accept that marriage meant a fresh and total life together."

3. Draw a sharp line between the time spent living together and being married.

Although this assignment requires more than a honeymoon, it is still a good place to start. A honeymoon does the best job after living together if you select a spot new to both of you. The key to this fresh start is to go after experiences that you have not shared before. Look for the new, don't rely on the old. Learn how to heighten the excitement and novelty of matrimony even after years of living together.

Some brides and grooms have been known to separate for a week before the new beginning of their lives. The most unusual suggestion, which called for unique fortitude, was from Kimberly and Mark. I was on the other end of the phone when Kimberly whispered to Mark, "Do you care if I tell her about the three months before our wedding?" He must have given her a signal to go ahead. "For three months before our wedding we stopped having sex," Kimberly said giggling. "We wanted sex to be special again when we got married, and it was."

Moving into a new home or redecorating calls for less of a sacrifice than Mark and Kimberly but are noteworthy tactics nonetheless. So are Seth's resolutions to be more helpful and supportive of Theresa. After the honeymoon he awakened early each day to pack her lunch for work and have dinner ready when she stepped through the door after a night of graduate school classes. A number of couples reserved date nights or weekdays just for each other.

Give your marriage a fresh start. Don't shortchange the fun that can be in store for you. Tammy's husband didn't. He carried her over the threshold of their old apartment, and then he began a wildly creative sex life that lasted for seven months. Tammy hardly thought it possible to infuse their sex life with such impassioned love and lust. Her intuitive groom, however, obviously believed otherwise. "Billy made a real effort to find new places for us to have sex in the house. We christened the stairwell, the kitchen counter, the closet—anywhere he could think of." Her husband made such a tasty beginning to their married life that Tammy reciprocated with candlelight dinners that she still serves up regularly years later.

DON'T BE THROWN BY PROBABLE CHANGES

Recognize that the marriage you have entered into requires your understanding and energy. Former live-in lovers may initially be remiss in their reply to the question "What changed after you got married?" and respond, "Nothing." However, upon further questioning they often relent and point to obvious changes, some good and some bad. One to be aware of and get rid of quickly is a sudden onslaught of possessiveness, which can create an acute case of claustrophobia in your partner. Just as harmful is settling so comfortably into your new state of matrimony that you begin to take your partner for granted.

Undoubtedly there will be new demands placed upon you by family members and your mate. Jackie laughs, "All at once I was married to his family, too." There will even be new problems to challenge you. Diane said that although she and Harvey had lived together for a few years, once they married they encountered a rough spot that lasted two months. "I could tell that Harvey was experiencing a temporary panic over finding himself married. I just let him ride it out."

There is no escaping the complexities of love and marriage. But making a concerted effort to pave a smooth way from living together to matrimony should afford your love relationship a much better future.

CHAPTER 11

The Necessary Art of Self-Protection

Don't shortchange yourself. You may need to protect your interests before you move in, even though only a handful of men and women I interviewed entered into some form of cohabitation agreement. Of those who did, the contract generally was in response to jointly buying property. Many unsuspecting live-ins harbor misconceptions about their rights and misperceive their partners' intentions, which all too often spells trouble. There is no reason to emerge a loser after live-in love if careful attention is paid to the information in this chapter.

MAJOR MISCONCEPTIONS

Three major misconceptions need immediate clarification lest they entrap live-in lovers and later embroil them in costly, lengthy legal battles.

Misconception 1: There is no reason to have a cohabitation agreement.

There may not be a reason when you lovingly move in together, but when emotions flair and tempers erupt in the face of splitting up, love's best intentions may fall short of fair play. By then, distorted points of view make it too late to strike an amicable agreement. In fact, the longer a couple lives together the greater the potential explosion when love ends. Sandra and Henry, an educated Yuppie duo in their mid-thirties who lived together for three years, are typical. Neither considered that there was anything to lose by moving in together. Years later, however, a trivial fight resulted in Henry filing criminal charges against Sandra.

Two Sides to Every Story: Sandra's Side

"I was naive about the kind of chances I would be taking by selling all of my household items and making two moves to two new cities to live with Henry. I never considered a legal agreement," says Sandra, explaining that she had known Henry a long time and had no reason to doubt him. He had always been extremely generous and loving.

"I never dreamt that after three years he would give me two weeks to get out of his house and wouldn't want me to take something as trivial and inexpensive as a potpourri burner that he'd purchased for me. When I left Henry's house, I left with my clothes and a few small items, though I had put about $3,000 into the house in paint, wall coverings, and odds and ends. Of course, there was no way to recover the paint and wallpaper or the cost of them. I had absolutely no place to live and no money to set up my own apartment. In fact, just a few weeks before I left, I had given Henry my $600 tax refund because he said that I needed to help out more. While we were living together I wrote him a monthly check for $250 that I suppose you could say was for rent. I also paid a few of the smaller incidental bills like my long-distance calls."

Feeling vulnerable, frustrated and angry, Sandra wanted what she felt was rightfully hers: a $2,000 grandfather clock that was a gift from Henry. "When we split, I could have tried to get a hell of a lot more money from Henry by saying that he owed me compensation for putting my career on hold. I could have said we were common-law partners," Sandra argues, correctly noting that the two states they lived in acknowledged this type of marriage but failing to understand that she and Henry did not fulfill the necessary criteria. "All I really wanted was the clock. I went to an attorney, but he told me to forget it, that it wouldn't be worth trying to get a few items for the legal fees I would incur."

Coincidentally, when Henry came knocking at Sandra's door two years later, she was in the process of making arrangements to finance the purchase of her own grandfather clock. "I knew he was living with someone else when he called me. It was like my revenge had been met," Sandra admits with a hit of pleasure in her voice, adding that she had declined his persistent pleas for more than a month. "When I left, I had told Henry that he would be sorry someday. It was a joy in a sense to know that he was running back to me. What happened is that I got caught up again in the lavish gifts, outfits, and purses, and his talk about the big house we would have and the country club we would belong to. Even though I knew I was totally nuts to go back with him, I was so overwhelmed that within months I picked out my wedding dress.

"When we talked about my quitting my job and moving out of town again to join him, I wanted to take some precautions. I was giving up so much, and the first breakup was so ugly. This time I wanted to be assured that I would be taken care of if we broke up. It had taken me a year to get back on my feet, relocate, and get a good job. If we lived together outside of marriage and anything happened to the relationship, I wanted Henry to set me up in a home or apartment and pay for all of the moving expenses. I think I stipulated a minimum cash figure of $2,000. Henry was very defensive when I gave him the agreement."

Sandra was correct to have misgivings about Henry's intentions. Apparently he floats in and out of relationships with women, not at all certain about his commitment but preoccupied with making sexual conquests. Once he got Sandra back in bed, his interest seemed to wane. Their romance took a drastic turn before the appointed date of Sandra's spring move. "I wanted to go to Boston for New Year's Eve to be with friends, but Henry was upset that I wasn't coming to visit him, so I changed my plans and decided to drive to New Hampshire to be with him. The Sunday before New Year's he left a message on my answering machine that our relationship was over, that it wasn't going to work, and that he wouldn't be back from his skiing trip out west until Sunday after New Year's. In the back of my mind, I said, 'He isn't going to get away with this again.' My anger had been aroused, and I was determined this time to get what was mine. I had not thought about taking the clock until then. I called him back several times before he would speak with me. When we finally spoke, I told him that I was coming to New Hampshire anyway to see mutual friends and wanted to stay in the house. I asked him if it would be okay." Whether Henry answered yes or no is a matter of dispute. Henry's neighbors are the ones who handed Sandra the key to his home.

What is certain is that when Henry returned home, he found the clock, some fine china, and a new set of costly luggage missing. He called the police and pressed charges for grand theft. "At first I was frightened," Sandra admits, "but then I got an attorney and told him I would fight for the clock, even though he recommended I return it and buy one for myself. 'Why should I?' I asked him. 'I already had one of my own.' If Henry hadn't pursued me again, I never would have had the opportunity to get these items. This time I was not going empty-handed."

Henry's Side

"It rubbed me the wrong way that Sandra wanted an agreement before she would move in," Henry says, his objections reflecting the sentiments held by other live-ins. "Here we are coming into a relationship, and she is banking on it to fail. I didn't see our relationship as risky for her either time, she did. If she moved in with me and something happened, like I died before we got married, she wanted the right to stay in the house until it was sold. She wanted my estate to pay her approximately $7,500 [a different figure from that given by Sandra] and give her the grandfather clock. And in the event she quit her job, moved in with me, and I called off the wedding, she wanted $7,500 and the clock. There was no way in hell that I would sign an agreement like that. That was ridiculous. She only wanted to get something out of the relationship for herself."

According to Henry, though, this wasn't the only stumbling

block that caused this on-again, off-again relationship to take a final tumble. "Several months after we got together for the second time, we had a big argument about setting a wedding date and about whether or not to have kids. I told Sandra to let it go. I had two children from my previous marriage, and I wasn't having any more. I wasn't ready to commit to a wedding date, either. Sandra kind of backed off, thinking that I was stressed out about work. It's my fault. I should have told her in September that I didn't want to get married even in a year and that we'd come to an end.

"I did let her know that I was going out with another woman and kept making excuses for months why I couldn't see her and why I couldn't afford to send her a plane ticket to visit me. I made it clear that we wouldn't be spending Christmas or New Year's together, but then she called and told me she was taking time off work to drive the nine hours to be with me for New Year's. I left a message on her answering machine that she shouldn't come because I was going skiing in Utah and wouldn't be back for New Year's. She called my hotel room in Utah in the middle of the night and wanted to know what was going on. I told her I was not coming home and just to let it go. I don't know why she started getting really mad. She said she had made plans to meet other friends and needed a place to stay. I told her that I really did not want her staying at my house and asked her why she couldn't stay with her friends. In the meantime, she call my neighbor and said she had been given permission to stay at my house, which wasn't true, and they gave her the key. She left two messages for me, wanting to know when I would be home and saying she would pick me up at the airport and cook me dinner before she started her drive home. I called her back at my house, but she wasn't in, so I left a message telling her that I would be home late Sunday."

Obviously Sandra didn't meet his flight. "When I got home, I knew Sandra had taken the things from my house to get even with me. Sandra thinks the clock is hers. She did pick it out and it was her idea to buy it, but she wasn't living with me when I purchased it for the house. She had gotten a truck and moved the clock out in the middle of the night. Her attorney made her return enough of the stolen items to reduce the charge from grand theft to a misdemeanor. Now he is arguing that this is not a criminal matter but a civil suit having to do with a property settlement. He has threatened to sue me with malicious prosecution if I continue to press the charges of theft. It's hard to believe that I ever trusted Sandra."

Pointing out that his loss is minimal, Henry says his friends have advised him to forget the clock and drop the charges. He hasn't yet decided what to do. Can you imagine what would happen to couples when the stakes are higher?

Misconception 2: Because we live together, we can be considered common-law marriage partners.

When circuit ministers and judges made infrequent visits to towns in the early American pioneer days, common-law marriages—a carryover from English law—were recognized to protect women from being taken advantage of by men. Today, however, common-law marriage is an option for a limited number of men and women who cohabit, and it is no longer associated primarily with low-income couples. It is surprising how many men and women who live together are misinformed about what constitutes this type of marriage. Many men and women do not live in states that recognize common-law marriages, yet they believe that their time spent together as a couple constitutes wedlock by law. To clarify incorrect impressions, pay close attention to the following facts:

1. The District of Columbia and only thirteen states recognize common-law marriages. These states are Alabama, Colorado, Georgia, Idaho, Iowa, Kansas, Montana, Oklahoma, Pennsylvania, Rhode Island, South Carolina, Texas, and Utah. In October 1991, the Ohio legislature rescinded common-law marriages. Laws do change, and couples should check the current position of the state they live in before they consider themselves common-law partners.

2. Common-law marriages are not valid in most states unless a couple (1) declares an intent to be husband and wife, (2) conducts their lives as spouses would, and (3) holds themselves up to the community as a married couple.

3. Age requirements and length of cohabitation required to assume the status of common-law partners vary by state. A law professor at the University of South Carolina says merely writing a one-sentence declaration of a couple's matrimonial bond on a piece of paper can legally bind them under his state's common-law status. In fact, in 1989 a woman who lived with actor William Hurt for five weeks in South Carolina filed a $10 million suit in a New York court on the grounds that they became common-law partners during that period.

4. Common-law marriages are subject to many provisions of traditional unions and are legally dissolved through divorce or death.

5. The status of the common-law marriage cannot be conveniently adopted by one partner after a breakup just to attempt to obtain a better settlement.

6. Common-law partners who seek the court's assistance in settling disputes that arise when their union ends bear the burden of proving the validity of their marriage. The cumbersome problems and judgments inherent in this process were the motivating forces behind changing Ohio law to recognize only those marriages performed by clergy or other specified individuals. To substantiate the claim of common-law partners, individuals must have evidence that they presented themselves as husband and wife such as having received mail together or having filed joint tax returns.

A highly publicized common-law suit involved Winfield Scott, a player for the New York Yankees, and Sandra Renfro, a former flight attendant with whom he had a daughter. Renfro claimed that she and Scott, together from 1982 to 1985, were common-law partners under Texas statutes. Renfro was able to prove to the court's satisfaction not only that Scott was already married to her when he took his formal vows with another woman, but also that she was entitled to $1.6 million dollars. Scott, who appealed the case, was nonetheless ordered by the court to pay Renfro's $210,000 in lawyers fees and monthly alimony of $10,000 until the case was settled.

Misconception 3: Your interests as a live-in partner are protected by law.

The infamous suit of *Marvin v. Marvin,* which introduced the concept of palimony in 1976, has contributed to a false sense of security, particularly among female live-ins. It is time to replace fact with fiction. Few, if any, of the guaranteed rights that protect the interests of spouses seeking a just and equitable divorce settlement—such as alimony—apply to live-ins.

1. The implications of *Marvin v. Marvin* will not necessarily impact the settlement you seek after live-in love ends. However, let's take a look at the claims made by Michelle Triola Marvin, actor Lee Marvin's six-year live-in companion. Michelle sought monetary compensation for the years she put her own career on hold to provide Marvin not only with sex and companionship but also with numerous other household and social benefits. This exchange of services was supported by Michelle Marvin's claim that Lee Marvin had stated to her, "What I have is yours, and what you have is mine," and implied an inherent contract in their live-in relationship.

The case was eventually heard by the California Supreme Court. While the court awarded Michelle $104,000 in "rehabilitative alimony," this decision was later reversed and she never received any of the settlement. Legal experts point out that the significance of the case lies in the fact that the court determined the right of live-in partners to sue for a legal settlement. Remember, this decision was confined to California, and palimony per se has hardly become a guarantee in settlements across the country.

A recent court decision in Madison, Wisconsin, upheld Linda Walsh's claim that her live-in lover of eight years owed her $6,000 after they split because the house they lived in appreciated by $16,500. The suit was not made on the basis of an argument for palimony but on the grounds that her partner, Harlan Ray, was "enriched" by her contribution. Walsh's attorney argued that although Ray owned the house and made all of the improvements himself, her client contributed by cleaning up during construction and providing workers with refreshments. The District Court of Appeals upheld the lower court's decision despite the fact that Walsh made no financial contribution and that Ray helped support her and her children during the eight years she lived with him.

2. *The law that applies to live-in relationships and settlements is still evolving.* Without an existing body of law, John A. Carnahan, past president of the Ohio State Bar Association and an active member of the Family Law Section of the American Bar Association, says that there are no guidelines for court decisions. This makes it difficult for anyone to be absolutely certain how the courts will respond when hearing these cases. To emphasize how far the United States is from garnering a uniform response to live-in settlements, it is interesting to realize that cohabitation is actually *illegal* in Arizona, Florida, Idaho, Illinois, Michigan, Mississippi, New Mexico, North Carolina, North Dakota, Virginia, and West Virginia.

The stigma of living together outside of matrimony has noticeably lessened, but the laws to protect participants are lagging behind social acceptance. And where laws do exist, they are inconsistent. The United States has not yet equaled Sweden, where living together has become institutionalized and live-in arrangements are subject to legal guidelines. In the United States matrimonial law was founded to protect the family, and living together has been viewed by the courts as a sexual arrangement that goes against this "public policy." Those who lived together outside of the legal bonds of matrimony were expected (1) to do so at their own risk, (2) without the legal protection afforded traditional marriage partners, and (3) without a legal basis for compensation. In other words, a live-in partner has no right to demand alimony or automatically share in property if the relationship ends. This is precisely why in the past it has been possible for a woman to live with a man for as long as thirty years and still have no legal claim to his estate or the home they shared.

3. Because a large number of men and women who live together have been divorced, it is very important that they be aware of anti-cohabitation laws that discontinue their ex-partner's responsibility to pay alimony. Alabama, California, Connecticut, Georgia, Illinois, New York, Oklahoma, Pennsylvania, Tennessee, and Utah have statutes pertaining to this issue.

4. There are visible gains, particularly in the posture of the courts to recognize and enforce a contractual agreement between individuals who live together. According to the authors of *The Spousal Equivalent*, couples living in Georgia, Illinois, and Louisiana should be aware: These states do not enforce living-together agreements. On the other hand, Kansas, Minnesota, and Washington have assumed a more liberal posture empowering the courts to determine fair live-in settlements.

THE LIVING-TOGETHER AGREEMENT: QUESTIONS YOU SHOULD ASK

Living-together agreements are worth exploring. Before you and your partner determine whether or not you want to pursue this avenue to protect your interests, consider the following questions:

Question 1: What is a cohabitation, or living-together, agreement?

A living-together agreement is a formal contract between two parties not covered by matrimonial law. The agreement should be a written document that bears both individuals' signatures. For the agreement to hold up in court, the contract must be entered into freely, without coercion, and with full disclosure. If a dispute arises and the court is asked to enforce the conditions of the contract, it is adjudicated according to contractual, not family, law.

Question 2: What should be included in the contract?

The living-together agreement should be a comprehensive contract that spells out each individual's responsibilities, including financial participation within the relationship and terms of dissolution. Carnahan believes that soon there will be a checklist of all items that need to be covered in cohabitation agreements, as currently exist for the increasingly popular premarital contract. In the meantime, consider these points to cover in a contract designed to foster an equitable separation should the relationship end:

- determination of ownership of capital items
- determination of distribution of items and property
- responsibility and settlement of debts
- monetary value and compensation of services exchanged
- arrangements for children and pets
- responsibility for legal fees incurred in split
- determination of ownership of season tickets
- settlement of joint leases.

This partial list should be an indication of the intricacies involved in ending a live-in relationship.

Question 3: Who should have a cohabitation agreement?

Whether you elect to create a formal agreement should not be based solely on your personal wealth. A live-in relationship that ends without a written agreement can be more costly than a divorce and accrue $15,000 in legal fees, according to Johnette Duff and George G. Truitt, authors of *The Spousal Equivalent*. With this in mind, everyone should seriously consider putting this safety net in place.

If an all-inclusive agreement seems unnecessary, there are individual circumstances that should not proceed without a contractual agreement. For instance, if one pays for one's partner's education or assumes total responsibility for household costs during that period, an appropriate agreement might state how and when one would be compensated if the relationship fails. A written contract should be prepared when taking loans or purchasing a house, property, or other significant items together. An agreement should specify the joint terms of ownership and detail how that property would be disposed of in the event one party died or wanted to buy or sell the property and needed to determine a price. If children are born of the live-in relationship, it is important to obtain a written custody and support agreement.

◆ ◆ ◆

Question 4: Do you need a lawyer to prepare a cohabitation agreement?

"Anyone can act as his own attorney," Carnahan explains, cautioning, "While it sounds simple enough to write your own agreement, many individuals think they are covering all the bases, and they aren't." If you appoint legal counsel, Carnahan says, it is an "ethical requirement" that each individual obtain his or her own lawyer to represent his or her interests. If this is not done and the court is asked to enforce the stipulations of the contract, one party can easily plea that he misunderstood the terms of the contract or was coerced into signing, thereby nullifying the agreement.

An attorney is equipped to determine according to recent judgments how a state might look upon such contracts and whether they will be viewed as being counter to "public policy." The state of legal flux prohibits anyone from assuming that creating a cohabitation agreement is a simple matter.

OTHER MEANS OF SELF-PROTECTION

Not everyone is comfortable with a cohabitation contract. Fortunately there are other ways to obtain limited protection:

1. Establish a joint account only for household expenses and separate accounts for all other monies and investments.

2. Retain receipts and maintain records of gifts and joint purchases.

3. In the event that children are born of the union, establish paternity. Without it, a child may be denied due support and a share of an eventual inheritance.

4. Prepare a will, carefully plan your estate, purchase life insurance, or establish a trust to protect yourself and your partner.

5. If you want your partner to act on your behalf in the event that you become medically or mentally incapacitated, it is necessary to grant a "Power of Attorney" to your partner before that time. Your lawyer will be able to provide you with the necessary documents.

NEW TRENDS

The entire issue of gay and lesbian couples is having a impact on the interests of unmarried heterosexual couples. A "domestic partnership" is a new concept developed largely to accommodate same-sex couples. The truth, however, is that a large proportion of the people taking advantage of this policy—whether it be to obtain employee insurance benefits, student housing, or a legal registration of their live-in relationship—are heterosexual couples. Those who fall into the category of domestic partnerships generally must (1) live together, (2) be financially interdependent, and (3) demonstrate a stable and intimate partnership. The domestic partnership, however, has little effect on major issues that affect both heterosexual and homosexual couples.

THE IRONY OF ANOTHER LEGAL WEB

Many men and women who live together in the United States attribute the appeal of their lifestyles to the absence of legal ties. Ironically, many of these same individuals will later seek assistance from the courts to protect interests similar to those of married couples. Whatever the rationale, the point is clear: Men and women need to consider the serious financial implications of cohabitation before they put their names side by side on the mailbox. Taking this precaution will in turn make moving out and moving on easier to handle if and when live-in love comes to an end.

CHAPTER 12

Moving Out, Moving On

It is time to move out? Need some tips on how to move on? Before you can make that fresh start, you must acquire the right attitude, tend to old business, and regain control. Following the game plan compiled from the lessons learned by men and women who have faced the end of live-in love will inevitably help you survive your own traumatic split.

WALKING THROUGH A BREAKUP STEP BY STEP

The following five-step plan is dedicated to Sherrie, who through a fog of tears and breathless sobs said during our interview: "I need someone to tell me how to get on with my life. I can't even put on a necklace without remembering how great it felt having Ned hook it for me while we dressed for a night out together." Although she was the one left behind, perhaps if she had asked herself the questions in Step 1, she would have realized the futility of trying to make Ned a lifelong partner, and his exit might have been a little easier to accept.

Step 1: Deciding It's Over

The first assignment is a tough one. It took Scott months of contemplation. "I have done a lot of soul searching since we talked," he told me when I called to check on the progress of his live-in relationship. "It won't work with me and Claire. She isn't right for me."

Scott was moving in the right direction. It was the same path that Hannah took a few years ago. "You have to decide what it is you want and then be determined not to settle for anything less. I was twenty-five years old and had been living with Bruce for three years when I realized I wasn't anywhere near where I thought I would be at that age. I didn't want to break up, but I couldn't go on the way things were. Bruce could have gone on living with me forever. I wanted something different. I definitely wanted to get married. For me it was a matter of choosing a lifestyle. If Bruce wasn't going to get married, I wanted to go out and find someone else. I was pretty realistic after I asked myself what I wanted from this relationship, and I knew I wouldn't get it from Bruce. That may sound cold," Hannah acknowledges, "but I knew in the long run what would make me happy."

If you need more ways to realistically evaluate the status of your relationship, try some advice from Barbara DeAngelis. In her book, *Are You the One for Me?*, she offers a set of considerations for any couple, whether they are living together or not, that may help you determine whether your relationship is ready for the finale. It might be time to lower the curtain if you decide:

1. You are not compatible.
2. The sexual chemistry between you is weak.
3. You and your lover are growing in opposite directions.
4. Your lover has serious personal problems.
5. Your partner is unwilling to work to make your relationship better.

If this describes your significant other, your feelings, or your relationship, you might need to resolve to move out. The next step will help propel you in that direction.

◆　◆　◆

Step 2: Preparing for the Breakup

Preparing yourself and your partner emotionally and mentally for the break is tricky and requires a great deal of self-control. But the benefits are worth it.

Is breaking up ever really a surprise? Rarely. Your own experiences in relationships and those in this book should all validate that answer. Diane Vaughn, a sociology professor at Boston College and author of *Uncoupling: Turning Points in Intimate Relationships*, has found predictable patterns in disintegrating relationships that unravel over time. Vaughn maintains that the partner who wants to leave the relationship begins a "psychological departure," which is frequently overlooked by his or her significant other. Inadequate expressions of discontent by the departing partner and misreading of this behavior by the other partner prevent the real trouble from readily surfacing. Consequently, when one partner announces the intention to leave, the other individual, who has failed all along to recognize the signs of an ailing relationship, feels as if this is a sudden and unexpected breakup.

This process has been well-documented by many of the live-in lovers in this book. Katherine, for one, says, "It took me a year to leave. When we were in the process of buying our house I knew it wasn't right, because I had severe anxiety attacks. I was fighting it because I had a lot invested into the relationship and I didn't want to give up my house or face the pain of separating. I wasn't happy, but I didn't come out and tell Chris right away. When I did begin to express myself, I wanted to go to therapy, but he didn't. Finally I got so fed up that all I could think of was getting away. He was so angry that he wouldn't give me anything that was rightfully mine. I left in such haste that it cost me all my interest in the house. Looking back today, I wouldn't have done it the same way. I shouldn't have been such a wimp."

Katherine's own unhappy ending clearly demonstrates the importance of being able to openly and assertively deal with a relationship that is falling apart and the need to prepare for the breakup.

◆　◆　◆

Coming Up with a Strategy

Accept the fact that you will suffer some discomfort, pain, and unhappiness when you split. Daphne Rose Kingma, a marriage and family therapist who authored *Coming Apart,* wrote, "Next to the death of a loved one, the ending of a relationship is the single most emotionally painful experience that any of us ever goes through."

It is rare for someone to feel as good as Belinda did after she broke off with Ray and moved out. "It felt great. I was so relieved that I went out to breakfast and felt on top of the world," she recalls. "Breaking up wasn't traumatic for me because I knew I had done the right thing. It was harder for Ray."

Even Buddy, who wanted out of his two-year-long relationship with Gloria, admitted to pangs of unease. "I was happy when we broke up, but then I went back several months later and said, 'Well, maybe we could work things out.' I think my male ego was a little hurt that Gloria hadn't come running after me. When I rang her doorbell one night and she came to the door with her blouse unbuttoned and didn't invite me in, I actually became sick to my stomach. The whole breakup made me physically ill."

Some men and women suffer bouts of serious depression, prolonged spells of crying, withdrawal, and grief. "I don't think you can avoid the pain," Peter Hall says after ending a seven-year relationship. "We were both hurt, but we managed the pain."

Try to exit with as little conflict as possible. Proceed cautiously and keep your live-in partner's feelings in mind.

"It takes guts to get out before more damage is done," Steven says. "In order not to throw out all of the friendship, respect, and caring you have built up over the years, you have to be honest with each other. If you stay together when you really don't want to, things can get nasty and chew up each other's self-esteem. Why destroy the good feelings you still have about each other?"

Steven wishes he had followed his own advice. He and Eleanor fought it out for more than a year, exchanging hurtful verbal blows born out of frustration. Numerous other men and women admitted to sexually rejecting their partners long before they moved out and witnessing the emotional and psychological damage this caused their live-in.

An abrupt departure can, however, be just as hurtful as a long and arduous one. The best rule of thumb is to try for an amicable settlement by proceeding as swiftly as possible while allowing time to tie up loose ends. Otherwise you may end up feeling as William did: "Patty and I never really talked about breaking up or how we felt. We got into a huge fight, and I left in anger. I'm not sure that's the best way to end things. I haven't spoken to her in a year, and it still bothers me not knowing what happened to the love we shared," William says remorsefully.

Activating the Plan

"After two years of carrying the burden of the relationship and doing everything, I threw the ball in Billy's court. He couldn't carry it sexually, socially, or emotionally. He was never able to say, 'I love you,' or be a real partner. I was afraid of being alone, but after I realized that Billy didn't know how to love, being alone seemed preferable to being with him any longer. It was a traumatic day when I moved out," Sara says. "I don't know how I could have gotten through it without a plan."

Sara's plan is worthy of attention:

1. "Talk to your partner and tell him or her when you are planning to move out," Sara suggests. "It provides a transition period for both of you."

2. "Call a friend and let them know you are having a problem and need their help. Setting up a support system before you leave is something I failed to do after my first live-in experience ended. That made it much more difficult for me to handle. This time I asked Freddy, a friend for many years, to be with me that day. I knew I couldn't be alone. Leaving was ripping my heart out."

3. "Convince yourself that you can stand on your own and that you will be okay. Have a place to go and money in your pocket. It will help you feel more secure," Sara concluded, noting, however, that despite financial security the first three months were practically unbearable until she determined to get on with the healing process.

Step 3: Beginning the Healing Process

The key to the healing process is to adopt a positive attitude and make recovery your goal. Here are some ways to accomplish just that:

1. Sara suggests, "You have to take the bull by the horn and have the inner strength to tell yourself, 'I am more important than anyone else in the world.'" Without realizing it, she was doing exactly what therapists advise: Repair your own self-image, which was most likely bruised in the breakup.

2. "Absolve yourself and others from blame," Carolyn advises. "My mental outlook became healthier when I decided to forget that I didn't see the break coming or that I felt betrayed. None of that did me any good. Stop blaming the other person and look at what you can do to help yourself. Otherwise you won't start healing."

3. "Put away the guilt," is Howard's tip. He acknowledges that he felt terrible and guilt-ridden breaking up with Sally after moving her away from her hometown. It took a long time for him to stop feeling responsible for her and begin getting on with his new life.

4. "You have to allow yourself to cry and talk about it," Lenny advises. "At first I tried to keep all of the pain to myself and would go out to parties and bars and get drunk. It started to affect my work. A good pal made me move in with him and spent hours talking to me. In a few months I was in good enough shape to move into my own place and focus on my work." If you need a counselor instead of a good friend, don't hesitate to find a qualified one.

5. "Begin to explore new options and avenues for growth," Linda says. Men and women both recommend meeting new people, going to new places, trying a new activity, or taking a stimulating course. Holly agrees, "I needed to put more constructive thoughts into my head. One that I kept remembering came from a book called *How to Survive the Loss of a Love:* 'Don't just settle for surviving and healing. Use this experience as a springboard for greater growth.'"

6. "I pampered myself with visits to the spa and little gifts," recalls Sally. "It made me feel better. I even took a vacation with a

friend. After a breakup it is time to do things in a way that pleases you. There is nothing wrong with catering to your own whims for a while."

7. Find pleasure and satisfaction in being self-reliant and alone after your partner moves out. Johnny did. He plunged into bachelorhood and turned into a gourmet cook. "I really enjoy this," he says with sincere enthusiasm for his newfound culinary skills.

Ruth Ann found it relaxing to march to her own beat instead of Mark's for awhile. "I got to liking the fact that I could eat what I wanted and go where I wanted *when* I wanted without having to worry about anyone else. Things are going just fine on my own," she reveals.

8. "Moving into a new and bright apartment was important to my frame of mind," Susie says. "I made sure that my surroundings would be upbeat and pleasant to come home to." That was a good idea. Women who stayed in their apartment or home after the split also recommend a little redecorating. I suggest starting with the bedroom.

9. "There is no way that Gail would have been able to break it off with me unless she moved out of town," Tip says, admitting she made a wise move. Make sure you are far enough away for your separation to work. Don't dangle temptation in front of your nose.

10. "I needed to get out and go on dates as soon as I could," Ed says. "I was less miserable out with another woman than at home, knowing Sara was with her new boyfriend." However, *when* you reenter the dating scene is an individual matter. The consensus among men and women was to take a little time off from dating and give yourself some breathing room before you get back into circulation. Move into the social scene when you are ready to enjoy other people's company and when you are able to control those urges to vent your unhappiness and anger over your split on a date.

11. "Break the emotional attachment," Valerie says with strong emphasis. "Stop deliberately recalling romantic and now-painful memories. Don't frequent restaurants or vacations spots you went to with your significant other. Stop driving by his home or going places where you think you will conveniently bump into him."

Tim couldn't move on until he put away all of Kelly's letters.

"I didn't want to let go of anything," he admits. A year later he is much happier now that these love notes are no longer in his possession.

Step 4: Accepting That It Is Really Over

Accepting the fact that the relationship is over for good is one of the most difficult steps in moving out and moving on. Consequently, numerous men and women deny this painful reality and prefer to believe that Jane or Jim will come back. Taking this posture prevents them from productively moving ahead and wastes time and energy on fruitless dreams of winning back his or her love. There seem to be three questions that these jilted lovers keep asking themselves, and they need some honest answers.

1. "How can I be sure it is over for good?"
There isn't a definitive test that will determine the future or completely answer this question. While most men and women who initiate the split do so with the intention that it will be permanent, some, like Kent, change their direction. "I guess that when I asked Julie to move out after living together for two years, I was initially trying to get rid of her and regain my freedom," Kent admits after a little prodding. "It wasn't until we both thought that our relationship was over that I realized that wasn't what I wanted either. Just a few weeks after Julie completely refused to see me at all on a casual, uncommitted basis, I proposed."

Unlike Kent, most live-in lovers who break up do not come running back into each other's arms. The romantic tales of the ones that do comprise but a small number of happy endings. The majority of live-ins waiting for their lovers' return are more likely to fit Maggie's sorry description. "When Kip moved out, I thought he would come back in four or five months. When he didn't return, I talked myself into giving him seven months. After a year, I finally began to accept that he wasn't coming back and emotionally eased myself out of waiting for him," Maggie recalls candidly.

In view of the evidence, the most realistic advice from those who have pined away in the shadows waiting for a lover's return is to assume unequivocally that he or she is not coming back.

2. "Would dating each other after the split help us get back together?"

In most cases the answer is no. Dating tables the conflict, prolongs the indecision, and delays coming to necessary conclusions even though it may be temporarily soothing.

Patrice admits, "It was very emotional when Bo and I moved out of our apartment into separate units after a year of living together. We both felt committed and in love. We even expressed wanting to get married, but never at the same time. So we decided to date but not live together. Knowing that our relationship would continue in some way made it easier to separate." P.S.: The relationship did continue, but only for a short time. Other, less decisive post live-ins drag the dating game on for years, creating a whole new stalemate.

Charles wanted to do just that when he asked Martha, his ex-live-in, to go out again. "He wanted to put the relationship back to exactly the same place it had been; that was basically with no commitment," Martha explains. "He didn't say, 'Let's get married.' We dated for another full year before I finally said, 'That's it. We're not getting anywhere.' I felt he needed time. That's what I gave him and then I said goodbye."

3. Are there signs that we might get back together again?

If your ex-lover is actively pursuing you after fleeing the premises, that is indeed an optimistic sign. It is a more meaningful and trustworthy indication of his or her sincere intentions if he or she previously treated you with genuine respect and love. In fact, assert Beetie Youngs Bilicki and Masa Goetz, authors of *Getting Back Together,* unless that core of love and caring is still intact after the split, there is little hope for a meaningful reconciliation.

Step 5: Extracting a Lesson

Once you regain control over your emotions, it is time to look at the loss of love more objectively and evaluate what was right in your relationship and what went wrong. Extracting something positive from the experience lessens the bitterness and resentment over investing so much time and energy into a love relationship that fails.

Turning the breakup into something more positive enhances the healing process and paints a brighter picture of the future.

Although Lou spent several years with Emmy in a troubled relationship full of emotional turmoil, he nonetheless feels that he benefited from the entire experience. "I think I truly found myself," he says. "I didn't know what I wanted out of life in terms of marriage, but after living with Emmy I have a much better perspective. I know that I want to get married and think I have a clearer idea of the kind of woman with whom I want to share my life. At least I will be able to take that with me to the next level of a relationship when I look for a partner."

Jennifer says that while she wishes she had never lived with Chuck and suffered his abuse, it taught her something. "I learned that I need to have boundaries and set limits on how people treat me. I will never accept treatment like that again."

Many live-ins vow never to make the same mistake again. Paula admits that she was like many women: too compromising, too trusting, and too easy the first time she moved in with a man. "I realized I let people take advantage of me and felt like a failure when Benjie moved out. I decided to change things, so I got in my car, moved to Florida, and found a job. When I met Jim—a couple of years younger than me—in an exercise class, I wasn't even looking for a relationship. I was more interested in being friends than lovers but was flattered by his obvious interest. I could feel my confidence rising again.

"Several months went by before he asked me out," Paula continues. "I felt extremely comfortable with him, and when our relationship became more intimate we would sit on the bed all night and talk. It was important for both of us to get all the skeletons out of the closet about previous disappointing love relationships and our insecurities. I was able to tell Jim that I knew I had a tendency to be too giving and that this time I wanted someone who had the capacity to return that kind of love, not take advantage of it. Talking through all of my fears made us closer and helped me learn to trust him when he said he loved me. Even though we were deeply committed to each other after several months and it would have been easier and more economical to let him move in, I didn't until we were officially engaged and had a wedding date set. I needed to be sure that he wouldn't leave me. We have both worked hard to make what we feel in our hearts grow." Paula is now a happy bride.

Roxanne had moved in with Sly when she was fresh out of college and before she had the opportunity to discover how well she could do on her own. Living with him excused her from making her own decisions or relying on her own judgment. They married but divorced within a few years after Roxanne found the arrangement suffocating and uncomfortable. Shortly after the split, she met Pete and became madly attracted to him. Nevertheless, Roxanne knew what she needed, and it wasn't another live-in—not at that moment anyway.

"I absolutely wanted to have a place that I could call my own," she announces with conviction. "It was my starting over place. I wanted to establish my own identity. Once I found out who I was, I asserted myself more than I ever did in my other relationship. This made things with Pete better from the beginning. He moved in, but not until I had my life under control and I was firmly convinced we would marry," she proudly reports a dozen years after they tied the knot.

Molly played out her new relationship totally differently because of the lesson she had learned. "When I moved in with Tom it was because I was hesitating about marriage. I wasn't sure if I should marry him or if we would be compatible. What I realized when it was all over was that all of my uncertainty about him meant that I must have known he wasn't the right man for me. If I had listened to myself I wouldn't have had to move in to find that out. All living together did was delay the point of decision in our relationship. I don't look back, however, and say, 'Oh, I made a terrible mistake because it didn't work out.' Instead when I met Al I said, 'I won't repeat that experience with him.'

"Al and I started dating two years ago. I was thirty-two and he was thirty-seven. He did ask me to move in but didn't press it. He knew exactly what my sentiments were on the subject. There wasn't any reason for me to live with him. I felt confident that I could find out by dating him if we were compatible and whether I wanted to marry him, and I have. Now I am sure that we will be happy when we marry in six months. I have no reservations whatsoever."

MOVING OUT OF THE TRAP ZONE

Successfully progressing through this five-step plan is the last lesson in *The Living Together Trap*. Completing the telling journey through these twelve chapters and carefully examining the revealing relationships should have alerted every reader to the potential dangers of live-in love. Being aware, realistic, introspective, and cautious is the only way to avoid the trap that has gripped so many in the throes of live-in relationships. Taking all the information given and applying it to your love relationship can and will encourage thoughtful, productive decision making that protects your interests and nurtures your future happiness. Certainly that is what everyone who has participated in this project wishes for each reader who faces the prospect of whether to move in, move on, or move ahead in finding lasting love.